Confessions of a...
COFFEE BEAN

THE COMPLETE GUIDE TO COFFEE CUISINE

MARIE NADINE ANTOL

SQUAREONE
PUBLISHERS

Cover Designer: Phaedra Mastrocola • Cover Photo: PhotoDisc, Inc.
Text Illustrator: Kathe Cobb • Typesetter: Gary A. Rosenberg • Editor: Joanne Abrams

Square One Publishers • Garden City Park, NY 11040 • 516.535.2010 • www.squareonepublishers.com

Permission Credits

The photos on pages 2, 48, 49, 51, 53, and 56 were reprinted courtesy of Jim Lohse, amsterdam-holland-travel.com.

The photos on pages 3, 4, 19, 22, 54, and 72 were reprinted courtesy of Starbucks Coffee Company, © 2002 Starbucks Coffee Company.

The photo on page 40 was reprinted courtesy of Starbucks Coffee Company, © Borislav Iochev 2002 Starbucks Coffee Company.

The photos on pages 25, 73, and 86 were reprinted courtesy of the Colombian Coffee Federation.

Library of Congress Cataloging-in-Publication Data

Antol, Marie Nadine.
    Confessions of a coffee bean : the complete guide to coffee cuisine /
Marie Nadine Antol.
        p. cm.
      ISBN 0-7570-0020-7
    1. Coffee. 2. Coffee brewing. 3. Cookery (Coffee) I. Title.
      TX415 .A55 2002
      641.3'373—dc21

                                                        2001007689

Printed in the United States of America

10   9   8   7   6   5   4   3   2   1

Contents

For Mr. Chris

This book is dedicated to
Christian M. Westerdahl, my gorgeous son-in-law,
who has as much appreciation for
fine coffee as I do.

With love from your MIL

Preface

Throughout my early years, my parents had an ongoing dispute over the merits of coffee versus tea. It was a genial argument tinged with amusement as each tried to convince the other to switch beverages. I suppose it was her English heritage that caused my mother to insist on tea, while my father, of stern Scottish stock, had to have coffee. I never thought much about it growing up, but now I wonder just when and why my father switched from tea to coffee.

Perhaps the bantering between my parents over the delights of both beverages was something of a blessing, because today I have a deep appreciation for both tea and coffee. Mother took her tea with lemon and Father took his coffee with cream, but my "cuppas" were diluted with milk. I grew up drinking milky tea with my mother and what we all called "coffee-milk" with my father.

The first time I was allowed coffee was a momentous occasion. I must have been about six or seven. I remember feeling very grown-up when Father said I might have coffee with him. In those days, electric coffeemakers were few and far between. Father's coffeepot was a percolator that simmered on one of the back burners of the stovetop. He poured about an inch of hot fresh-brewed coffee in a cup for me, added a spoonful of sugar, and filled the cup with milk. I loved it immediately.

As I got older, the proportions changed and, somewhere along the way, I graduated to coffee with cream and sugar, which is how I drank it for a very long time. As a young adult, I remember dashing into the building where I worked, eager to escape swirling snow and cold winds, and stopping in the coffee shop for coffee-to-go. This was long before espresso, cappuccino, or caffè latte made the scene. It was just a cardboard cup of very ordinary coffee with sugar and a dash of cream. With my gloves stuffed in the pockets of my coat, I clutched the cup between my chilled hands and welcomed the warmth on the ride up in the elevator. That first sweet and creamy sip at my desk was pure pleasure.

After the birth of my first child, I decided it was time to take my coffee black. Not only did black coffee seem more adult somehow, but I didn't need the extra calories I was taking in with the addition of cream and sugar. Those were the days when cream was cream. We didn't use half-and-half; we used the real stuff, and low-cal "pretend" cream substitutes were still years in the future. Back then, my coffeepot was still a percolator that sat at the ready on one back burner. I poured myself a cup, carried it to the den, and put it on the coffee table. Then I sat on the floor and started sipping. Hmmm. Was the coffee bitter, or was I just missing the mellowing that came with the sugar and cream? I persevered. Sip after sip after sip. I finished the cup and went back for more.

Knowing what I know now, I'm sure that coffee was bitter and over-brewed. It was our custom to start a potful in the morning and leave it on a low flame to keep it hot. As the morning wore on, the coffee must have become very stale, very bitter, and, eventually, even scorched. Fortunately—or unfortunately—I didn't know the difference, and no one else did either. When researching this book, I discovered that Americans came late to an appreciation of fine coffee.

At any rate, I've been taking my coffee black for over forty years now, and—for me, at least—I think that's the only way to truly enjoy a cup of fine coffee. When there's no dilution, the subtle differences in the flavors of specialty roasts and gourmet coffees really come through. I still brew a full pot of coffee every morning, and I still drink it until the pot's dry. The difference is that I treat myself to some of the finest coffees in the world now, and I decant the fresh brew into a vacuum pot so that it holds its flavor. Every delectable sip is as rich and delicious as the first.

Because of my life-long love affair with coffee, it seemed a natural step to write a guide to coffee cuisine. In addition to my years of enjoying coffee in the United States, I had "sipped" my way across Europe, learning about the many ways in which coffee is prepared and celebrated in various countries. Armed with this firsthand knowledge, I had a head start on my research as well as a true appreciation of the coffee bean.

I began my research with great enthusiasm and ended up surrounded by books from the bookstore and library, as well as masses of printouts from the Internet. Every source I consulted provided fascinating facts that were new to me. By the time I had finished wading through all the material, I knew I had extracted every secret the coffee bean had been hiding. I'm delighted to pass them all on to you in Part One, "The Life and Times of the Coffee Bean."

The recipes that appear in Part Two, "The Tastes and Pleasures of the Coffee Bean," came from a variety of sources. Many of them are from a collection I started years ago, some came from family and friends, others were adapted from the very old cookbooks I've treasured for a long time, and still others I worked out myself. My goal throughout was to present you with the best collection of coffee drinks and coffee accompaniments found anywhere. My family was delighted when I began testing the recipes—although some were more of a success than others. Don't worry, though. I gave you only the best and tossed away the rest.

If you're not already a coffee aficionado, I'm betting that you'll become one by the time you've finished this book. Coffee has been called an affordable luxury. For pure pleasure, I invite you to sample the gourmet coffees of the world, as well as the many delicacies, from croissants to crème brulée, that can enhance your enjoyment of the coffee bean. I promise you'll find favorites that will add a touch of luxury to every day of your life.

Introduction

Coffee has been my friend for a long, long time. During our years together, the coffee bean has told me many secrets—secrets about its origins, about its world travels, about its irresistible charms, and about much, much more. Finally, I decided it was time to share what I'd learned with other coffee lovers. And so I began my work on *Confessions of a Coffee Bean*.

Confessions of a Coffee Bean has been designed as a fascinating tour of the wonderfully enticing world of coffee. You're going to discover so many incredible secrets in this book—secrets that will amaze you, delight you, and even amuse you.

Part One, "The Life and Times of the Coffee Bean," opens with a fascinating look at the history of coffee. Chapter 1 starts with the legend of Kaldi, the Abyssinian goatherd who was the first to sample coffee's pleasures. It then moves through the centuries, culminating with coffee today.

Chapter 2 is where you'll learn all about the coffee tree—how it's grown and where it thrives—as well as how the fruits of the tree are harvested and roasted, ultimately ending up in your home. You'll even discover why coffee is justly called an "affordable luxury."

Chapter 3 focuses on the coffeehouse, starting with the beginning of these popular establishments in Arabia and continuing with a jaunt through Europe. Of course, this chapter wouldn't be complete without a look at the coffeehouses of North America, including America's most famous coffeehouse, Starbucks.

Chapter 4, "Coffee and Your Health," may be the most eye-opening chapter of all. You probably know that some people must avoid caffeine. But are you aware that both caffeine and other coffee bean components can actually be beneficial? In Chapter 4, you'll learn that coffee can help fight cancer, help relieve asthma, and boost both alertness and mood. In fact, the coffee bean is more of a friend to the body than you might ever guess.

Chapter 5 gives you an in-depth and personal introduction to some of the most amazing coffees that are available today, taking you from the sublime to the ridiculous in the world of the coffee bean. If you've been content with com-

mercial coffees to this point, I think this chapter will spur you to visit your local specialty shop and try a gourmet blend or two. And if you're already interested in fine coffees, this chapter will acquaint you with some rare and wonderful beans that you may want to add to your shopping list.

Chapter 6 is where you'll learn just about everything there is to know about making a great cup of coffee. You'll begin by selecting beans, a coffeemaker, and perhaps even a coffee bean grinder. Then, you'll put everything together and, with the help of some guidelines, brew a perfect pot.

Part Two, "The Tastes and Pleasures of the Coffee Bean," is an eclectic collection of recipes for both coffee drinks and coffee accompaniments. First, Chapter 7 teaches you how to make a wide variety of coffee beverages, from steaming brews like Café au Lait to icy concoctions like the Espresso Shake.

Then, Chapter 8 provides a bevy of desserts and other coffee companions, from the luscious Sacher Torte to coffee-kissed creations such as Rich Coffee Tiramisu and Creamy Coffee Cheesecake. You'll even find recipes for coffee-laced candies and sauces.

As I said, the coffee bean has been my friend for a long, long time, so it has been a true pleasure to celebrate its wonders within these pages. I hope that *Confessions of a Coffee Bean* helps you better understand and appreciate the world of coffee, and guides you in forging your own rewarding relationship with the wondrous coffee bean.

PART ONE

The Life & Times of the Coffee Bean

CHAPTER 1

Coffee Through the Ages

Coffee is the common man's gold, and like gold,
it brings to every man the feeling of luxury and nobility.
Where coffee is served, there is
grace and splendor and friendship and happiness.
All cares vanish as the coffee cup is raised to the lips.

—SHEIKH ABD-AL-KADIR, 1587

The coffee plant and its rosy fruits first came to the notice of humans in Kaffa, Ethiopia, sometime in the third century, CE. And the rest, as they say, is history. From nearly the moment of its discovery, the coffee plant was valued and hoarded; planted and nurtured; sold, traded, and even stolen. It was brewed as an aromatic beverage, it was prized as a medicine, it was used to curry favor with kings and courtiers, and, more than once, it was nearly banned as a dangerous stimulant. The amazing story of coffee's rise from an unknown plant to an international phenomenon is the subject of this chapter.

THE LEGEND

Most experts agree that it was around the third century when the extraordinary powers of coffee first came to light in Abyssinia, known today as Ethiopia, in the province of Kaffa. It was this province, of course, that gave coffee its name. Here's how the legend goes.

One day, a lonely Abyssinian goatherd named Kaldi went searching for his wandering goats. Night was falling. He was tired and he wanted to get the goats home and into the fold so he could have supper with his good wife. It had been a very long day, and Kaldi was drowsy from the heat. He heard his goats bleating excitedly somewhere in the distance. He couldn't imagine what they were up to, but he followed the sounds and found them munching on some small reddish fruits he had never seen before. The animals were frisking and frolicking in a patch of shrubs, making their way from one bush to the next, bleating and eating as they went. Kaldi saw that his goats were full of some kind of super-charged energy, and he couldn't help but laugh at their antics. "Well," thought the goatherd, "it certainly seems that these berries are making my goats very happy. I'm going to try some of these strange fruits myself."

Kaldi plucked a berry and nibbled off a bit. The flesh of the berry was tender and juicy, but not very flavorful. He saw that there were two green seeds inside. "Well," he thought, "my goats are eating the whole fruit, and so will I." The seeds seemed tough, but Kaldi had strong teeth. He popped the rest of the berry into his mouth and crunched down, chewing mightily. By the time he had eaten several more of the fruits, the goatherd realized that he no longer felt tired. In fact, he felt so good that he was tempted to dance along with the goats, but he still wanted his supper. He filled his pouch with the berries. It took him awhile to get the goats on the road home. In fact, he had to give a couple of them a good clout with his stout stick before they would stop munching on the rosy fruits.

The discovery of coffee is credited to a third-century Abyssinian goatherd named Kaldi, who noticed his goats frisking and frolicking, full of energy, after they'd nibbled the rosy fruits of the coffee plant.

After trying a few of the berries herself, Kaldi's good wife shared his enthusiasm and said, piously, that the fruits must truly be a gift from God. "Tomorrow," she told Kaldi, "you must pick some of these miracle berries and take them to the monastery. The monks should know of these wondrous fruits." Kaldi knew she was right, so he carried a pouchful of berries to the monks the very next day. It is written that the monks were greatly inspired after they partook of the rosy, red fruits. They became ever more diligent in their devotionals, and were even more eager and energetic at their work.

While researching this book, I discovered that everyone who has anything to say about coffee relates this little folk tale. Although some accounts attribute the discovery of coffee berries to a shepherd, not a goatherd, I just couldn't imagine sheep frisking and frolicking. Goats, yes. Sheep, no. Sheep graze and have a placid disposition, while goats are adventuresome, curious critters with a reputation for investigating everything and eating anything. Let that be the final word on the subject, coffee lovers. Our gratitude must go to Kaldi and his nosy, noisy goats.

All good stories conclude with "The End," but for coffee, this was just the beginning of an epic saga. It took many hundreds of years for coffee to travel from Abyssinia to the breakfast table of the average American. Let's continue this remarkable journey.

THE OLD WORLD

Now that you have read the legend of Kaldi, you know that the story of coffee began in northeast Africa, where an excited goatherd discovered the plant and introduced it to very appreciative monks. Soon, the monastery became famous for the spirited praying of its coffee-inspired residents. And eventually, the demand for coffee spread throughout the Old World.

The Beginning

Historical records show that there was a thriving trade between Yemen and Africa as early as the fourth century. Authorities say that it was most likely traders who brought coffee to the interior of Arabia sometime in the sixth century. It is written that, early on, the beans were soaked in boiling water and the energizing drink that resulted was much appreciated. The beverage was called *gahua* or *qahwa,* which means "that which prevents sleep."

By the year 1000, evidence shows that not all the beans were brewed into a sort of tea. At least some of the green beans were planted, and eventually, coffee plantations were established at the southern tip of the Arabian Peninsula, primarily in the countryside surrounding the city of Mocha, Yemen, just across the Red Sea from Ethiopia. The trees thrived and coffee became an important export; Mocha soon was a very busy port of call for merchant ships. A trader described it in these words:

> The city is very populous as it is filled with merchants from the many cities of Islam and The Indies. Because of the staple [coffee], there be thirty-five sailing ships crowded into the harbor, alongside freighters from Suez.

Early on, *mocha*—like *kaffa*—was a common name for coffee. Both of these names, of course, were derived from the places where the sought-after beans originated. Mocha's importance to the coffee trade declined with the opening of the Suez Canal in 1869. Today, we recognize mocha not as a major player in the world of coffee, but as the name of a delicious combination of coffee and chocolate—a result of the chocolate aftertaste for which Mocha coffee beans are known worldwide. (You'll learn more about the different coffees of the world in Chapter 5.)

The ancient city of Mocha is where the historical thread unravels. It starts up again several centuries later. Here's what I picked up, a tidbit at a time, to provide a more complete picture of the story of coffee.

The 1400s

For a very long time, only Africa and Arabia grew *Coffea arabica,* the earliest cultivated species of the coffee plant. By the fifteenth century, Arabia was exporting coffee beans to North Africa, the eastern Mediterranean, and India. Arabian merchants were especially jealous of their coffee trade and went to great lengths to protect their monopoly. To prevent other countries from growing their profitable product, merchants had the beans parched before exportation, rendering them infertile.

No one seems to know just when the green beans were first roasted or when coffee, as we know it today, was first brewed. However, it seems likely that people eventually noticed that the parched beans made a richer beverage than the fresh beans. It may have been only a short step from parching to roasting.

Sometime in the mid-1400s, coffee made its way to Constantinople, crossroads of the known world, where it was embraced by the Turks. In the private households of the wealthy, coffee was carried to the salon by servants with slippered feet bearing coffee services on brilliantly lacquered trays. The brew was served in tiny exquisite cups, the finest being the Finjan cups from China, with small, elaborately chased silver spoons alongside. Silk napkins finely embroidered with strands of silver and gold thread completed the picture.

In 1453, a coffee shop—the Kiv Han—opened its doors for business in that most cosmopolitan of cities. Records shows that this was the first true coffee shop anywhere. The Turks still love their coffee. (For more information on Turkish coffeehouses, see Chapter 3.)

The Turks valued coffee so highly that they passed a law making it grounds for divorce if a husband refused coffee to his wife.

The 1500s

By the late sixteenth century, European travelers had discovered the "secret" brew so prized by the eastern world, and wrote of coffee in their travel journals.

Coffee had established itself as an important food in one corner of the world. But as the sixteenth century dawned, it would become apparent that not everyone loved the beverage. Even more important, throughout the 1500s, news of the "secret" brew would begin to spread to other portions of the globe.

It was in 1511 that the governor of Mecca, Khair Beg, tried to outlaw coffee. He somehow got it into his head that coffee was too popular, and imagined that its stimulating properties would energize the opposition. What he hadn't counted on was the fact that the sheikh himself was hooked on the stuff. The sheikh had Khair Beg beheaded.

Travelers to coffee-loving countries soon began sampling the brew, and their writings relate their delight. Leonhard Rauwolf, a German adventurer who visited Constantinople in 1573, wrote a passage in his journal attesting to his pleasure upon tasting coffee for the first time. A few years later, in 1580, Prospero Alpinus, a botanist and physician of Padua, Italy, wrote a book in which he recalled his first sight of a coffee tree while visiting foreign lands, and mentioned the "decoction" made with the fruits of the tree. Although the coffee bean itself had not yet travelled to Europe, word of it was beginning to leak out.

The Sufis of Yemen considered coffee a blessing that was given to man to help him better execute his religious duties. Although it's certain that the Sufis had been performing a ritual involving coffee for many centuries, it was in the late 1500s that this practice came to the notice of the outside world through the writings of one Abd al-Ghaffar. This is how the ceremony was described:

> They drank kaffa every Monday and Friday eve, putting it in a large vessel made of red clay. Their leader ladled it out with a small dipper and give it to them to drink, passing it to the right, while they recited a ritual phrase such as, "There is no god but God, the Master, the Clear Reality."

The beloved "kaffa" had certainly invaded all areas of life—even religious observance. But it was the leader of another group of believers who would help make coffee the favored beverage of Europe.

The 1600s

Sometime in the early 1600s, a merchant of Venice wrote home, "The Turks have a drink of black color. I will bring some with me to the Italians." When coffee arrived in Italy, it soon became a sensation. No less a personage than the Pope was reportedly enamored of the brew. When devout Catholics urged the Holy Father to ban the drink on the grounds that it was a ritual beverage of Islam, the Pope refused. Instead, he baptized the brew, thereby legitimizing it and "converting" it to an acceptable Christian beverage.

In July of 1669, ambassadors of Mohammed IV, Sultan of the far-flung Byzantine Empire, traveled to Paris bearing gifts for the king. Along with silks and spices, the ambassadors carried several sacks of coffee beans, which were distributed among the king's favorite courtiers. Rich Parisians began making arrangements to import their own beans. Soon, all across Europe, ships' captains who sailed to ports of call in Arabia were inundated with orders for coffee beans.

Coffee was beginning to be more and more commonplace in the drawing rooms and salons of royalty, the aristocracy, and the wealthy, but the common folk had yet to have a taste. That state of affairs ended in 1672, when an enterprising Armenian merchant who made his home in Paris offered coffee to the public for the first time by dispensing steaming cups of the brew at the fair of St. Germaine. The exotic beverage was an immediate hit with the man—and woman—on the street.

Around the same time, a lame street merchant named Candiot began offering coffee on the streets of Paris. By all accounts, he was scrupulously clean

Venetian traders were the first to introduce coffee to Europe. Quickly, coffee became a sensation.

and neat and wore a spotless white apron that covered him from shoulder to shoes. With the help of his Arabian companion, Joseph, Candiot walked the streets crying out the wonders of the brew. Between them, they carried a coffeepot, a vessel holding burning charcoal to heat the pot, a pitcher of water, and a basket of serving cups and utensils. Parisians, eager to sample the exotic drink, made the venture a success.

No source seems quite sure how it happened or exactly when it occurred, but at some point in the late 1600s, Arabia lost its monopoly on coffee growing and exportation. (Note that although coffee also grew in Africa, Africa's coffee was not exported.) That's when Baba Budan, an enterprising trader of India, managed to smuggle out seven live coffee beans by binding them to his midsection with a strip of cloth. One source says that Baba Budan planted the seeds in a secluded place in southern India, near a village named Chikmagalgur. However the seeds made their way to India, the resulting trees flourished. It is written that coffee beans harvested from the offspring of the original seven seeds are known as "Old Chik," and that "Old Chik" beans total about one third of India's coffee today.

According to legend, Baba Budan, a trader from India, smuggled out the first live coffee beans from Mecca to India in the 1600s. The Arabian monopoly had been broken.

Indian merchants weren't the only ones who wanted to cut out the middleman and grow their own coffee. By the end of the seventeenth century, many countries were using coffee as both medicine and beverage. In 1690, the Dutch managed to smuggle a living coffee plant out of the port city of Mocha, Yemen. Not long after that, the Dutch established the first European-owned coffee plantations, one in Ceylon and another in their East Indian colony on Java. The Arabian monopoly had been broken.

The 1700s

As the eighteenth century dawned, coffee was no longer considered an exotic taste of the East. Rather, the robust brew was viewed almost as a necessity.

Everyone, it seemed, wanted their cup of coffee. And the law of supply and demand being what it is, the price of coffee beans was ready to escalate. Let's set the scene.

Because the Red Sea ports of Egypt were under the thumb of the Ottoman Empire, the Ottoman Turks, as rulers of Egypt, controlled much of the shipping trade. Although they had lost what amounted to a monopoly on their spice trade when the Dutch entered the picture, the Turks still had control of coffee exports coming out of Arabia, and they decided to capitalize on this good fortune. In an indignant letter written to a friend in the early 1700s, a Frenchman named Jean de la Roque analyzed the problem:

> The potentates of Egypt [the Turks] have become more difficult in letting that commodity [coffee] be transported, which has caused a scarcity and raised the price to six and seven haucks per pound.

The newly inflated coffee prices were considered unconscionable. Everyone agreed that it was becoming increasingly important to find an alternative source of the precious coffee beans. For both individuals and governments, wealth was represented by control of important commodities, such as sugar, tobacco, tea, cotton, and, increasingly, coffee. Holland, England, and France, the great powers of the day, wanted in on the coffee trade. Although by 1706, the Dutch were exporting beans from their coffee plantations established in Java and Ceylon near the end of the 1600s, their yield was small. Clearly, coffee was a commodity with a bright future, and the race was on to establish new, higher yielding plantations.

Even though the European climate was hostile to the fussy tropical plant, the Dutch managed to coax several trees to bear fruit at their Hortus Botanicus arboretum in Amsterdam. An account of the circumstances written by an informant of the times survives, as follows:

The Hollander told us there was a great Coffea tree of the species in the Hortus Botanicus of Amsterdam whose height was equal to a two-story house. This great tree originally came from Arabia, brought while very young, and transported to Java. After some stay there, it came at last to Holland, where it grew to perfection. The fruits of this tree have produced diverse young plants, some of which have borne fruit from the age of three years.

The Arbre Mère, or Mother Tree, was given to Louis XIV of France in 1714. And before long, her "babies" helped introduce coffee plants to the New World.

This was clearly a coup of great magnitude. However, the Dutch were not nearly so protective of their burgeoning coffee industry as the Arabs had been. Showing off, Amsterdam began currying favor by gifting certain privileged European aristocrats with coffee plants. The first, which was from the fruit of the famed great tree of the Hortus Botanicus, went to Louis XIV of France in 1714.

King Louis treated his new possession more as an ornamental curiosity than an opportunity to establish a French source of coffee beans. Nevertheless, the king had a house of glass built to protect the delicate tropical plant. Indeed, the Jardin des Plants of Paris was perhaps the first true greenhouse on record. In its new home, the coffee tree was carefully tended. And when it began to bear fruit, the seeds were used to start more plants—plants that were sent far and wide. So important was the progeny of this gift that as time passed, the tree was given the title of Arbre Mère, or Mother Tree. And it was the Arbre Mère that was instrumental in introducing coffee to the New World.

THE NEW WORLD

Before a range of internationally grown coffees became commonly available in North America, many people thought that coffee was solely a product of Latin America. But as you've seen, coffee plants were first discovered and cultivated in the Old World. The coffee plants that traveled to the New World had two main sources. First, as I've already hinted, some seedlings came from Louis XIV's celebrated Mother Tree. Second, a large number of today's coffee plants resulted from one stolen plant. (Really!) And how did coffee achieve popularity in the United States? Well, it all started in the colonies.

Coffee Takes Root in the Americas

When we last left Louis XIV, he was carefully tending the Mother Tree—a coffee plant that had been given to him by the Dutch. This plant is thought to have made a small but definite contribution to New World coffee production.

Some of the seedlings from the king's tree were hand-carried by clipper ship to the French-controlled Island of Bourbon in the Indian Ocean—an island known today as Reunion Island. The coffee produced by these seedlings was known as Bourbon coffee, and it is still prized today. Fertile beans from the Mother Tree were also transported to Brazil and Mexico. If grown in Brazil, that variety is known today as Santos beans; if grown in Mexico, it's called Oaxaca coffee. Still other seedlings were transported to French Guiana. And, of course, as the original seedlings bore fruit and gave birth to children of their own, the grandchildren of Arbre Mère found their way to additional sections of South and Central America, making the plant available to still more potential coffee lovers.

However, long before the fruits of Louis' coffee tree were old enough and plentiful enough to be harvested for their beans, a French naval officer by the name of Gabriel Mathieu de Cheu stole a young coffee plant. It happened in 1723. No one seems to know where this robbery took place. However, records show that de Cheu hand-carried the seedling to Martinique in the West Indies. Within a half century, there were 19 million coffee trees growing on plantations in Martinique. Pay attention now: According to legend, *90 percent of the world's coffee sprang from this single stolen plant.*

While some of the New World's coffee plants are the offspring of France's Arbre Mère, millions of coffee trees in the Americas—and a full *90 percent* of the coffee of the world— are said to have come from a single plant stolen in 1723.

Coffee Reaches the Colonies

Captain John Smith is remembered in history for two things. First, in 1607, he founded Jamestown colony in Virginia, the first permanent settlement on these shores. That fact is beyond dispute. Second, Pocahontas is said to have saved his life when her father, the great Indian chief Powhatan, was about to have him put to death. This pretty story has passed into legend, but cannot be verified and continues to be controversial.

Whether coffee travelled to the American Colonies with Captain John Smith or was brought over by later settlers, the beverage was embraced by colonists long before the Boston Tea Party made coffee drinking a patriotic activity.

I now wish to bestow upon Captain Smith yet another claim to fame. Some authorities believe that he's the man who brought coffee to the colonies. However, in the early 1600s, coffee had yet to catch on in England, so it's doubtful that the early colonists were clamoring for coffee. Captain Smith certainly encountered coffee in his travels, and perhaps developed a taste for it. Did he bring coffee to the colonies? It's possible, but unverifiable. We do know that the *Mayflower* set sail for the New World in 1620. One source I consulted said that the manifest of this famous ship listed a "wooden mortar and pestle used to grind coffee powder," so it appears that at least one family had acquired a taste for this beverage. Of course, any coffee initially brought to the New World by the first settlers soon ran out, but as time went on, the colonies received coffee from the London warehouses of the East India Company, which was founded in 1600 under a charter given by Queen Elizabeth I. Indeed, even after the colonies declared independence, the British company continued to supply them with coffee beans.

By the middle of the seventeenth century, coffee was officially the beverage of choice in the Dutch settlement of New Amsterdam. When the British took over and changed the city's name to New York in 1664, coffee continued to be popular, but tea was still preferred by the British settlers. However, by the late 1600s, it was apparent that coffee had gained in popularity. In 1681, colonists were complaining about the high price of coffee beans. William Penn, who founded Philadelphia in 1682, was dismayed at having to pay 18 shillings and 8 pence for a pound of green coffee beans. That works out to about $4.65, or 12 cents per cup. That may sound reasonable to us today, but 12 cents could buy a full meal back then.

In 1668, statistics show that coffee had become the favorite breakfast drink in New York City. But it wasn't tea that coffee edged out of first place as a favorite breakfast brew. It was beer. Not until the late 1600s did the first public establishment serve coffee in St. Mary's City, Maryland.

By 1668, coffee had become the favorite breakfast drink of New Yorkers, edging out not tea, but beer.

Our account of coffee in the colonies wouldn't be complete without a mention of the Boston Tea Party. In 1773, a number of colonists, poorly disguised as Mohawk Indians, swarmed aboard three ships anchored in Boston harbor. With whoops and hollers, they threw all the tea overboard in protest against the high tax on tea levied by the English king. That's when coffee drinking became the patriotic thing to do.

Coffee Remains the Beverage of Choice

As time went on, and the United States grew large and strong, so did America's love of coffee.

Pioneers traveling west in covered wagons always carried coffee. It was brewed atop two or three stones over campfires both morning and evening. In fact, from the 1800s on, whether pioneer, settler, cowboy, explorer, or homebound citizen, the shopping list always included coffee.

Eventually, coffee became so popular that some people began to worry about its stimulating properties. In 1820, those railing against alcohol decided to take on coffee. They wanted the government to ban it. Temperance advocates spoke out against coffee in public, and wrote articles warning of its "dangerous" effects. They printed and distributed "broadsides" (flyers) on the streets suggesting that coffee was toxic. The public was beginning to take notice, and coffee sales were falling off, but then the protestors made a fatal error. They charged that coffee was a sexual stimulant. That did it. Sales sky-rocketed. The anti-coffee campaign fell apart, and we've been drinking this stimulating brew ever since.

Coffee became so much a necessary part of everyday life that in the Mexican War (1846–1848), it was doled out to American soldiers. The practice continued throughout the Civil War (1861–1865), and it's been going on ever since. All of our fighting men and women have their daily coffee.

The men of the United States Navy have a different story to tell. It was Josephus Daniels, Secretary of the Navy from 1913 to 1921, who outlawed alcohol on board ship when he took office. Prior to that ruling, grog—a mixture of

The Coffee Break

The coffee break is so much a part of the American lifestyle that you may be surprised to learn that it doesn't exist—or, at least, that it doesn't exist formally—in a large number of businesses. You probably know that white collar workers have always been able to drink coffee at their desks, whether they carried it in or it was brewed in a corner of the office. Blue collar workers, on the other hand, are a different story.

Back in the early 1900s, laws were enacted requiring employers to give women, the so-called "weaker sex," a rest break in the middle of the morning, time to eat the midday meal, and another rest break in the afternoon. Thought to be made of sterner stuff, men were allowed time to eat, but were not given rest breaks. However, the Civil Rights Act of 1964 changed everything. Equality—between the sexes as well as the races—was the name of the game. But instead of giving men rest breaks equal to the women, breaks were quietly abolished. Employers were no longer required by law to grant a mid-morning and mid-afternoon break, whether for a "comfort" stop in the bathroom, a rest and a stretch, or a cup of coffee. Women lost their privileges and men gained nothing.

rum and water—had been the beverage served to sailors. That practice had been started by a British Admiral named Edward Vernon. Nicknamed Old Grog, Vernon had outlawed pure spirits on board His Majesty's ships in 1740 and decreed that they be watered down. Enter Joe Daniels. He's the one who mandated that coffee, not grog, be the beverage on all U.S. Navy ships. The sailors started calling coffee a "cup of Joe," and the term stuck.

Coming of Age

As you have seen, coffee has long been a much-loved American beverage. But for many centuries, just about any old coffee would do for most people. Then,

A cup of coffee became "a cup of Joe" when Josephus Daniels, Secretary of the Navy from 1913 to 1921, ordered that coffee—not grog—be the beverage served on all ships of the U.S. Navy.

It was a case of penny-wise and pound-foolish on the part of management. Although many studies, past and present, show that productivity actually increases among those workers who are given breaks, employers viewed breaks as paid "time off." When management multiplied the wages paid each worker during the twenty-minute break by the number of working days per year, they pronounced breaks prohibitively expensive.

It's really not much better today. Some labor unions have negotiated breaks for their members, and some enlightened employers do permit them, but for the most part, a coffee break simply does not exist for many blue collar workers. Only nine states—California, Colorado, Connecticut, Kentucky, Minnesota, Nevada, Oregon, Washington, and Wisconsin—have enacted non-gender rest-period laws, consisting usually of ten minutes every four hours. And in each of these states, there are exemptions and exclusions to the laws.

But whether or not the coffee break is a formally sanctioned event, every American knows that it is very much a part of the American way of life. From Mom and Pop luncheonettes to coffeehouses to roving coffee trucks, merchants strive to give the country's workers the coffee they want. And whenever they have the chance, workers pause to savor that small luxury that seems to fuel the nation's labors.

in the mid-1980s, American taste began to mature as a selection of quality coffees and premium roasts flooded the market. Soon, the gourmet coffee market took off, and there's no end in sight. Overall, the market grew from $270 million in 1984, to $750 million in 1991, to around $1 billion in 1994. It's close to $3 billion today, with 20 million American adults drinking gourmet coffee beverages every day, whether premium whole-bean varieties or espresso-based beverages. You'll learn more about American coffee trends in Chapter 3, "Coffeehouses." For now, suffice it to say that the country's love affair with coffee—an affair that started even before the nation became a political entity—is going strong.

We've come a long way since the days when only the wealthy and privileged had access to the rich taste of coffee. Now coffee is available all over the world, and even people whose income is modest can afford the "luxury" of a well-brewed cup. This is truly remarkable considering the many processes involved in producing the final roasted coffee bean. Chapter 2 provides a closer look at the plant that has entranced people through the ages. It then follows the coffee bean on its extraordinary journey from crop to cup.

CHAPTER 2

From **Crop** to **Cup**

If you'll excuse me a minute,
I'm going to have a cup of coffee.

—APOLLO 11 ASTRONAUT TO JOHNSON SPACE CENTER,
HOUSTON, 1969

As you learned in Chapter 1, over the centuries, coffee was discovered and adopted by country after country, group after group. Although the settings may have changed and the method of brewing may have varied over time, the central figure in this odyssey—the coffee plant itself—remained essentially the same. This chapter will familiarize you with this ancient plant, from its fascinating structure to its painstaking cultivation and harvest. You'll learn about the all-important coffee cherries and the wonderful beans—actually seeds—that they enclose. And you'll learn how coffee beans are processed to yield the product that that you find in your local stores.

THE COFFEE PLANT

The coffee, or coffea, plant is a member of the Rubiaceae family. This is a very big family that includes more than 6,000 species of tropical trees and shrubs. Other well-known members of the Rubiaceae family include cinchona, from which we extract quinine; the gardenia; and bedstraw.

Carolus Linnaeus, a Swedish botanist, was the first to describe the genus coffea sometime in the 1700s. There are more than forty species of coffea, and some botanists disagree on exactly which plants belong in this genus and which should be excluded. All, however, agree that *Coffea arabica* and *Coffea canephora,* the latter of which is sometimes known as *Coffea robusta,* are the major players. Let's look at each of these varieties.

Coffea Arabica

As you may have guessed, *Coffea arabica* is native to northeastern Africa, although it is now grown in many different countries. This evergreen shrub may attain heights of twenty to forty feet in the wild, but when under cultivation, the plant is kept pruned to about eight feet to make it easier for pickers to reach the fruit.

C. arabica has glossy dark green leaves that are smooth and shiny on the upper side and paler below. The leaves can be up to two and a half inches wide and can grow up to six inches in length. In late summer, the plant puts forth dense clusters of fragrant white flowers that spring from the base of the leaves. The pretty blooms last only two days before giving way to the coffee cherries. These cherries, which are initially green in color, take from seven to eleven months to ripen, depending on both climate and variety. When ripe, the nearly one-inch-diameter oval fruits are a rosy red with two green seeds, or coffee beans, snuggly nestled inside.

The coffee plant is luxuriant, with deep green shiny leaves and, in season, clusters of fragrant white flowers. After pollination, the flowers are replaced by coffee cherries, each of which contains two coffee beans.

Arabica coffees are the premium coffees of the world, meaning that they are the most flavorful. They command a higher price than robustas, and are the coffees most often used in high-quality specialty blends.

C. arabica doesn't bear fruit until the trees are three to five years old. However, the obliging shrub continues to produce crops of coffee cherries for twenty to thirty years, with the beans becoming richer and more concentrated over time. A tropical plant, it prefers temperatures that range from the high fifties to the mid-seventies, and thrives in areas that have an annual rainfall of around sixty inches and an altitude between 3,000 and 6,500 feet. It is especially prolific in the tropics of South America.

C. arabica is the most widely grown species of coffee, accounting for about 70 percent of the world's coffee production. Arabica coffees are also the premium coffees of the world—meaning that they are the best—and are therefore among the most expensive. You may have heard of Jamaican Blue Mountain coffee and of Hawaii's Kona coffee, both of which are highly prized arabicas. (You'll learn more about the different coffees of the world in Chapter 5.) Arabica trees typically yield one to one and a half pounds of green coffee per year, and the beans contain about one percent caffeine by weight.

Coffea Canephora

Coffea canephora, which produces the popular robusta beans, is the second most important variety of the coffee plant. Like its arabica cousin, *C. canephora* can grow tall; if left to its own devices, it can attain a majestic thirty feet in height. But like the arabica plant, it is kept to about eight feet in height to allow for harvesting.

In other ways, too, the robusta plant resembles the arabica plant. *C. canephora* doesn't deliver a crop until three to five years after it is planted, after which the fruits take almost a year to mature. And the plant can continue to bear cherries for twenty to thirty years.

Like *C. arabica*, *C. canephora* appreciates sixty inches of rain per year. However, this plant likes it considerably hotter than its arabica cousin, and also tolerates higher humidity. Grown mainly in West and Central Africa, Southeast Asia, and parts of South America, robusta plants do best in equatorial conditions with temperatures ranging from the mid-seventies to the mid-eighties, and altitudes ranging from sea level to 3,000 feet. They also differ in that they are both more resistant to disease and higher yielding than robusta plants. The typical robusta tree yields as much as two to three pounds of beans per year—about twice the amount produced by an arabica plant. Moreover, at 2 percent caffeine by weight, the caffeine content of robusta coffee beans is higher than that of arabica.

If robusta coffee plants are not only hardier but also higher yielding than arabica plants, why, then, do they account for a smaller percentage of the world's coffee production? To put it simply, robusta beans are considered inferior to arabica because they are far less flavorful, with a distinct bitterness. This is why robusta beans are less expensive than arabica beans and are often used in lower-grade commercial coffee blends, as well as in the processing of many instant coffees, both flavored and unflavored.

Although robusta beans are inferior to arabica in flavor, the robusta plant is both hardier and higher yielding than the arabica.

Coffea Liberica

Before we conclude our discussion of the coffee plant, it's important to briefly mention *Coffea liberica*, which is grown chiefly in Malaysia and Guyana. Although a strong (parasite-resistant) plant, with fruits and seeds almost double the size of the favored arabica, *C. liberica* produces beans of inferior quality. Thus, liberica beans are grown primarily for local consumption and are seldom exported—although up to a decade or so ago, the coffee was appreciated by the Scandinavian countries.

Some Malays steep the leaves of *C. liberica,* much as tea is brewed. Interestingly, the leaves have even more caffeine than the beans. Coffea "tea" must be a potent beverage indeed!

GROWING COFFEE

Coffee is grown both on giant plantations and in the smallest of clearings. Under ideal conditions, compatible trees—banana and rubber trees, for instance—are situated near the coffee plants to shield the ripening coffee cherries from the full sun. Estate- and plantation-grown coffee crops are usually carefully fertilized and irrigated to insure conditions that foster optimum growth. Here's a quick look at the growing process.

The first step in getting a cup of coffee to your kitchen table actually starts when the ripe red cherries are collected and pulped, leaving the seeds behind. The fresh seeds, which are always taken from highly productive plants, can be planted immediately or dried for later use. Dried seeds can be stored for a year or more.

Whether fresh or dried, coffee seeds are pregerminated in indoor nursery beds. It takes from six months to a year before the tender seedlings are ready to be transplanted to the fields. To give them a good start outdoors, workers first prepare the ground by loosening the soil and grading the land. Coffee plants thrive where there is plenty of rain, but they need well-drained, nutrient-rich soil. While small, traditional farms may plant 400 to 1,000 plants per acre, large-scale plantations often space trees more densely, sometimes cultivating 1,500 to 4,000 plants per acre.

Once the coffee seedlings have been planted, they need to be carefully protected from diseases and pests. On traditional plantations, this means continuous weeding, the application of compost and mulch, and the introduction of pest-controlling predators. But coffee plants can fall prey to more than just pests. Sudden changes in temperature outside their preferred range can stunt growth and—although it's rare, given the tropical climates where most coffee is grown—an unexpected frost can damage or even kill the crop. You'll learn more about this in Chapter 5.

HARVESTING COFFEE

A frustrating fact for coffee growers is that coffee cherries ripen at different times on the same tree. One branch can simultaneously hold blossoms, green fruit, half-ripe berries, and rosy red cherries. That's why on most farms, the fruit of the coffee plant is plucked by hand, just as has been done since time immemorial. Pickers typically visit each tree three or four times in a season, picking only the ripe beans and leaving the green beans to be harvested at a later time. Even so, a good picker will harvest two hundred pounds of the fruit in one day.

But not all coffee picking is accomplished by hand. On large, modernized farms, common in Brazil, a harvesting machine is used to strip the tree of its fruit. Although these machines leave the coffee plant intact, they remove *all* the loose cherries—both those that are ready for roasting and those that are not yet ripe. But because such plantations operate on a massive scale, they are nevertheless able to yield a profit.

One branch of the coffee plant can hold blossoms, green fruit, and fully ripe coffee cherries, all at the same time. For this reason, on most farms, coffee is picked by hand to insure that only the ripest fruit is harvested, while the remaining fruit is left to mature.

PROCESSING COFFEE BEANS

As you've seen, up to a year may pass before newly formed coffee cherries reach full ripeness and are ready for the harvest. But that's just the beginning. Before the beans become a steaming cup of coffee, they must be extracted from the coffee cherries. Then they must be roasted. And in some cases, they must be decaffeinated. Let's learn more about how coffee moves from crop to cup.

Extracting the Beans

The fruit of the coffee plant is a many splendored thing. The beans are encased in five different layers. The *outer skin* that holds it all together is thin and a bit bitter tasting. When fully ripe, the *fruit* inside the skin is slightly sweet and very similar in texture to a grape. Next, there's a slick sticky layer, called *mucilage* for obvious reasons, which coats a tough paper-thin layer known as *parchment*. The final very thin layer is the *silverskin*, which clings to the beans for dear life.

It's not easy to release the beans from their five-layered prison, but it must be done. There are two means of performing this feat—the Washed Coffee Method and the Dry Coffee Method.

The Washed Coffee Method

The Washed Coffee Method is the more expensive means of extracting the coffee beans from the fruit, and the coffee it produces both looks and tastes better.

When an area has an abundant supply of fresh water, washing the coffee cherries is the preferred method. For obvious reasons, this type of cleaning—which, worldwide, is the most popular way of processing coffee—is also known as the Wet Process.

When the Washed Coffee Method is used, after an initial soaking in water, the outer skin and fruit are removed mechanically, leaving the beans behind. At this point in the process, the beans are still coated with the sticky mucilage that protects the parchment layer. The parchment is similar to the skin of an almond, but much more tenacious.

Next, the beans are soaked for twenty-four to seventy-two hours in fermentation tanks. The natural fermentation that occurs initiates an enzymatic action that loosens the mucilage and frees the parchment still clinging to the beans. This debris is then washed away with fresh water. Timing the process requires a knowledgeable eye. The beans must not be washed too soon with fresh water, or left to soak too long lest the quality be impaired. For the most part, the silverskin still remains, but don't worry. Some of it will be removed directly after the beans are extracted, and the rest will flake off during the roasting process.

Lastly, the extracted beans are dried, usually in the sun, but sometimes in mechanical driers. Washed beans generally produce a robust coffee with a higher acid content than that produced by the Dry Coffee Method. However, the Washed Coffee Method is the more expensive of the two processes.

The Dry Coffee Method

Sometimes called the Natural Method, the Dry Coffee Method first involves either allowing the coffee cherries to dry naturally on the tree, or picking them in the usual way and then laying them out in a single layer in the sun. Workers rake and roll the cherries around several times per day to insure even drying.

After the coffee fruits are dry, the pulp is stripped away with the aid of a mechanical hulling machine. Because the beans are at the mercy of the elements during this process, the quality of the beans may be uneven. At their best, these coffees have low acidity and heightened body and earthiness.

Sorting and Grading

No matter which method is used to extract the coffee beans from the cherries, once they have been freed from their encasing layers, they are sent through a mill that removes as much of the remaining silverskin as possible. At this point, the beans look pretty much like those you may have seen on display at coffeehouses and specialty stores. They are convex on one side and flat on the other, and have a long, furrowed line running lengthwise down their middles. Because they have not been roasted, their color is a cloudy yellowish-beige.

Now, the beans are passed through a series of screens with different size holes designed to grade them by size and shape. Next, they are graded by weight. Then, the beans travel along a conveyer belt, where workers with eagle eyes remove anything that doesn't belong, including broken beans, beans of the wrong size, and any pebbles that have sneaked in.

When the sorting process is complete, the beans are bagged in burlap sacks that are colorfully marked with the country of origin and the logo of the supplier. Each bag holds 150 pounds of the green beans.

Roasting the Beans

Roasting can either make or break the beans. Underroasting can yield a brew that is weak and flat, while overroasting can cause coffee to taste scorched and bitter.

After green coffee beans are bagged, typically, they are shipped to port cities in the importing country, where they are warehoused. In the United States, for instance, coffee is most often warehoused in New Orleans, although it is also stored in San Francisco, New York, and other cities.

From the port city warehouses, coffee is transported to individual roasting houses via either train or truck. The larger roasters are found in the coffee ports themselves, but nowadays there are also many smaller roasters, sometimes called *boutique roasters,* each of which may produce only a few hundred bags every year.

Whether coffee is decaffeinated or in its more natural state, it always makes a stop at the roaster before landing in your cup. This is because roasting releases the oils and acids that give each coffee its unique flavor. You may be surprised to learn that it's not the amount of coffee you put in your coffeemaker but the type of roast that chiefly determines whether brewed coffee is mild or strong. In fact, you might say that the roast is everything.

The Roasting Process

Coffee beans are usually roasted in large batch dryers, which spin and heat them evenly at temperatures that reach 550°F. During the roasting process, about 20 percent of the water content of the green beans evaporates and gases are released. In addition, the beans' starch content is converted to sugar. But the most important change is the one referred to earlier. The volatile oils and acids that give coffee its tempting aroma and delicious flavor are developed during the roasting process. In fact, if you ground green beans and used them to brew a pot of coffee, the resulting beverage would have no true coffee flavor.

The length of time the beans stay in the roaster is a critical factor. If the beans are underroasted, the brewed coffee is weak and flat in taste. If the beans spend too much time in the roaster, the coffee tastes scorched and bitter. This is why a roastmaster carefully supervises the entire process, monitoring the time, the temperature, the appearance and smell of the beans, and even the sound of the beans as they are heated. From time to time, sample beans are withdrawn and examined to further monitor the roasting process.

The Roasts

As explained above, the amount of time that the beans remain in the roaster determines the strength and flavor of the brewed coffee in your cup. To cater to different tastes, five different roasts have been developed. Here's a rundown, from very light to very dark. As you read the following descriptions, be aware that different roasters use different terms—many of which are included below—and define the roasts in slightly different ways.

Cinnamon Roast. In this light roast, the beans are typically roasted for eight or nine minutes—just until they turn tan and begin to "pop." The term Cinnamon Roast actually refers to the color of the beans at completion of the process. Other names for this light roast include Institutional Roast, New England Roast, and Half-City Roast.

The Cinnamon Roast is popular with coffee producers because it's fast, resulting in savings of time and labor. Moreover, the short roasting time prevents the beans from shrinking too much, which means a greater yield—which means more profit. However, this light roast doesn't fully develop the body and taste of the beans, leaving a low-body bean that's high in undesirable acids. To the educated palate, a Cinnamon Roast coffee may taste underdone and raw.

Regular Roast. A Regular Roast requires ten to eleven minutes in the roaster, leaving the beans a nice medium-brown. The flavor and body of Regular Roast beans are better developed than those of the Cinnamon Roast, and the acidity is high. This type of roast may also be designated as an American Roast, a British Roast, or a Medium Roast.

City Roast. In a City Roast—also called a Full City Roast, a High City Roast, or a Special Roast—roasting times of eleven to fifteen minutes yield beans that are a deep chestnut brown color. When brewed, the coffee taste is fully developed, with the sugars and acids nicely balanced.

Dark Roast. When beans are roasted from fifteen to eighteen minutes, the oil rises to the surface, producing beans with a rich, very dark brown color and a shiny appearance. This longer roast—which is also called a Double Roast, Continental Roast, or High Roast—fully develops the flavors, too. When brewed, the coffee is smooth, full-bodied, and rich.

French Roast coffee got its name many years ago, when the French used long roasting times to disguise the bitter flavor of African robusta beans.

French Roast. When beans are roasted for eighteen to twenty-two minutes, the result is the French Roast, also called the French Market Roast or Espresso Roast. This roast is characterized by very dark, almost black beans with a high shine, due to the development of surface oils. If you like an exceptionally strong, heavy-bodied, low-acid coffee, this roast is for you. Just keep in mind that at this point, no distinctive varietal flavor remains. In other words, the coffee has lost the flavor that distinguishes one bean from the next.

Blending the Beans

Although the beans from a single coffee may be sold unblended, in many cases, after roasting, beans from several different origins are combined to balance flavors. Some blends are classics. For instance, the Mocha Java blend—a combination of Mocha and Java coffees—has existed for centuries. Blending is used, too, to create "imitations" of coffees that are quite pricey—Kona coffee, for instance. While most people would hesitate to pay the high price charged for pure Hawaiian Kona, they might take a chance on a lower-priced coffee blended to taste like Kona. Finally, blending is important for national-brand companies that must produce coffees which are consistent in taste and price even as supply conditions change. Because of blending, every time you buy a specific brand, you know that you will enjoy the same coffee you've come to expect over the years.

Blending is used to create classic coffee mixtures; to make lower-cost versions of high-priced coffees; and to produce commercial products that remain consistent in taste and price even as crops vary and prices rise and fall.

Decaffeinating the Beans

Many people drink coffee specifically because of its stimulating effects. They enjoy the increased energy and alertness they experience after a cup of their favorite brew. (You'll learn more about this in Chapter 4.) But other coffee lovers find that a cup of Joe causes nervousness, irritability, and insomnia. For them, decaffeinated beans offer a satisfying and readily available alternative.

Be aware that because caffeine is a natural component of the coffee bean, it's almost impossible to get all of it out. Standards and regulations dictate the maximum amounts of caffeine that can be present in decaffeinated instant, roast, and ground coffees. In the United States, decaf coffees, in whatever form, generally have had at least 97 percent of the caffeine removed, although some brands remove even more. That's accomplished by one of two methods. Both methods use a decaffeinating agent to remove the caffeine from the green (unroasted) beans, but there is a difference. In the *direct process*, the substance comes in contact with the beans. In the *indirect process*, it does not. Here's how the two methods work.

Despite efforts to breed naturally uncaffeinated coffee beans, caffeine is a component of all coffee grown today. When desired, the caffeine is removed using decaffeinating agents ranging from water to substances such as methylene chloride.

The Direct Decaffeinating Process

In the direct decaffeinating process, the green coffee beans are first steamed—a step that softens the beans and loosens the bonds of caffeine. A decaffeinating agent is then mixed directly with the beans to leach out the caffeine. When that's accomplished, the beans are steamed or otherwise cleaned to remove the agent and then dried.

The Indirect Decaffeinating Process

In this method, too, green coffee beans are first steamed for the purpose of softening them and loosening the bonds that keep the caffeine in the bean. In the next step, the beans are mixed with water to leach out the caffeine. The water holding the caffeine is then separated from the beans, and a decaffeinating agent is added to the caffeinated water to remove the caffeine. The decaffeinated water is then reintroduced to the beans to put back flavor that may have been lost during the process. Finally, the beans are dried, just as they are at the end of the direct decaffeination process.

The Decaffeinating Agents

As you've learned, whether your coffee has been decaffeinated via the direct or indirect method, a decaffeinating agent has played a part in the process. If you use decaf coffee, chances are that you generally select a brand which says that it's been "naturally" decaffeinated. When the label says "natural," it means only that decaffeination was accomplished with an agent that is commonly found as a natural component of foods—although the label seldom tells you what the decaffeinating agent might be. That applies whether the direct or indirect process was employed. Here's a look at decaffeination agents, both natural and chemical, and a brief explanation of how each is used.

Charcoal or Carbon. Charcoal or carbon is used as part of an indirect decaffeinating process. First, steamed beans are soaked in water to extract the caffeine. The resulting solution, which contains both caffeine and various flavor and aroma elements, is then passed through activated charcoal or carbon filters to remove the caffeine. Then the decaffeinated extract is added back to the beans, restoring flavor.

Water. Water is used as the sole decaffeinating agent in only one method—the Swiss Water Process. In this direct process, steamed coffee beans are bathed in a water solution that is already saturated with essential coffee flavors and oils. Because of this saturation, the solution can't absorb any more of the flavor compounds in the coffee, and only the caffeine is removed. The downside of this method is that it extracts less caffeine than that removed by most methods—94 to 96 percent, as opposed to the usual 96 to 98 percent. However, the method leaves the all-important oils and flavoring agents intact. Just be aware that not all coffees labelled "Swiss Water Processed" have actually been decaffeinated using this method.

The Swiss Water Process is the only method that uses water as the sole decaffeinating agent. Although it removes less caffeine than that extracted by other processes, it leaves the coffee oils and flavor elements intact.

Ethyl Acetate. This might sound like something your dry cleaner uses, but it's not. Ethyl acetate occurs naturally in a variety of fruits—which is why this substance is often called a "natural" decaffeinating agent. Ethyl acetate is also produced commercially from two natural products, ethyl alcohol and acetic acid.

When ethyl acetate is the agent being used, the beans are first steamed, after which the ethyl acetate is added directly to the coffee. The ethyl acetate then leaches the caffeine out of the beans. The caffeine-infused solution is then drained away, and any residual amounts of the agent are removed either by heating the beans until all traces of the ethyl acetate have evaporated, or by first washing and then steaming the beans.

The Cost of a "Cuppa"

This chapter provides a clear picture of what goes into producing the beans that ultimately go into your morning cup of coffee. Considering all the steps involved—planting, tending, harvesting, sorting, roasting, and more—it's really quite amazing that coffee is so affordable, but most of us agree that it is. Statistics show that close to 70 percent of coffee drinkers in the United States think of coffee as an "affordable luxury." As a matter of fact, compared with other common beverages, coffee is downright inexpensive. Check out the following table, provided by the National Coffee Association. Just keep in mind that these prices reflect a national average and may not necessarily jibe with prices in your particular area.

Of course, coffee prices don't remain the same all the time. They change according to the laws of supply and demand. Anything that affects coffee growth—drought, too much rain, drastic temperature changes, an unexpected frost, or just plain nasty weather—can damage the crop and boost consumer prices. But when you savor your next cappuccino, remember that the beans in your cup may have passed through up to 150 hands and travelled thousands of miles. From that perspective, it is an affordable luxury indeed.

TYPICAL COST OF BEVERAGES SERVED AT HOME

Beverage	Average Cost Per 8-Ounce Serving
Coffee	$0.05
Beer	$0.44
Bottled Water	$0.25
Milk	$0.16
Orange Juice	$0.79
Soft Drinks	$0.13
Wine	$1.30

Carbon Dioxide. Carbon dioxide, or CO_2, is used in direct-method decaffeination. First, the carbon dioxide is liquefied under pressure and circulated through steamed coffee beans, dissolving the caffeine into the CO_2. Then, the carbon dioxide is drawn off, leaving the decaffeinated beans behind.

Methylene Chloride. This solvent is used in both direct and indirect decaffeinating processes. In other words, the steamed beans may be repeatedly rinsed with the agent, or the beans may be soaked in water, which is then drawn off and decaffeinated with the use of the substance.

The U.S. Food and Drug Administration (FDA) has determined that methylene chloride is safe for use in coffee decaffeination. Although the FDA permits up to 10 parts per million (ppm) residual methylene chloride to remain, in actual practice, the coffee industry's methods of decaffeination result in levels 100 times lower than this.

The Final Verdict

You've just read how, depending on the method used, decaffeinating agents can strip away not only the caffeine, but also the coffee oils and flavor elements. Usually, the process involves the return of these elements to the coffee beans. But despite this "return," just how flavorful is decaffeinated coffee? And how much do the inevitable solvent residues affect the taste?

Generally speaking, experts say that if you start with high-quality arabica beans—and not the lower-quality robusta beans so often chosen for decaffeination—the final product will still be quite flavorful. However, certain decaffeination methods tend to produce better coffee than others. For instance, some say that methylene chloride decaffeination maintains coffee flavor better than any other agent. The Swiss Water Process is also credited with maintaining true coffee flavor. As for the solvent residues, those miniscule amounts that remain in the beans following decaffeination are not believed to detract from the enjoyment of a good bean. However, the proof is in the cup, and many decaf drinkers sample several brews before finding one that meets their expectations.

Despite the dizzying number of steps that a coffee bean must take before it

Because caffeine has a bitter taste, its elimination need not spoil the flavor of the coffee. As long as high-quality beans are used, the final decaffeinated product should be rich and satisfying.

reaches your local stores, coffee remains both highly available and highly affordable. So the next time you yearn for a steaming cupful, don't hesitate to brew a pot in the comfort of your home. Or, if you prefer, visit your local coffeehouse—that friendly place where people meet for a great cup of Joe and, perhaps, some lively conversation. The next chapter discusses the history of these popular establishments where coffee lovers are able to relax, unwind, make friends, and share ideas, all while experiencing the delights of the coffee bean.

CHAPTER 3

Coffeehouses

Or to some coffee-house I stray,
For news, the manna of a day,
And from the hipp'd discourses gather,
That politics go by the weather.

—MATTHEW GREEN (1696–1737)

These days, many people view their local coffeehouse solely as a place to pick up a hot beverage and, perhaps, a bite of something sweet. But for centuries, the coffeehouse was far, far more. Originally, ladies were not welcome in coffeehouses, so all over the world, these establishments were popular meeting places for men, who gathered to discuss ongoing events, to conduct business, to argue politics, to champion causes, or just to complain about the sorry state of their lives. Some men even used the coffeehouse as a tool to further their careers, hoping to discourse so brilliantly that they would make a name for themselves.

As coffeehouses became more and more common, the clientele sorted itself by class and occupation, and men frequented those establishments where they felt most at home. Thus, counselors and judges might congregate at one coffeehouse, wealthy merchants at another, and college students and professors at still another. Similarly, men could often choose the atmosphere that most appealed to them, for while one coffeehouse might be characterized by lively debates over anything and everything, another might cater to a sedate crowd of elderly men who wanted nothing more than peace and quiet while they read their newspapers and sipped their coffee.

It is a testament to the worldwide popularity of coffee that the coffeehouse exists in so many areas of the globe. From Arabia to Austria, from Constantinople to the American colonies, the coffeehouse has flourished. And whether opulent or relatively bare, it has served to bring people together—for company, for intellectual stimulation, for entertainment, or just for the opportunity to savor a well-made cup of its customers' favorite brew.

ARABIA

Many of the coffeehouses of Arabia, Egypt, and other eastern countries were lavishly decorated with carved pillars, draperies of silk and velvet, and exquisitely tiled floors.

Long before the rest of the world became enamored of coffee, coffeehouses, called *Mokeya,* were common in Arabia, even in out-of-the-way places. If you will remember, coffee was once known as *mocha* because the Yemenite city of Mocha was the birthplace of the coffee tree. There appears to be a connection between mocha, the drink, and Mokeya, the coffeehouse.

The first coffeehouses on record are believed to have been established in Mecca, the holiest city of Islam, in the 1400s. Although they were originally gathering places for the devout, business dealings were commonly held there, as well. Some believe that public coffeehouses evolved from the ornate and luxurious rooms that wealthy Arabs and Persians set aside in their palaces especially to partake of the brew. Indeed, many Arabian coffeehouses—as well as many coffeehouses found in Egypt, Turkey, and other eastern countries—were lavishly decorated. Carved pillars divided the vast spaces into cozy nooks, and tapestries and elaborately patterned draperies of silk and velvet softened the walls. The men sat cross-legged on lush cushions placed on exquisitely tiled floors done in fanciful mosaics, or on high-backed banquettes piled with soft pillows. Most smoked tobacco through the slender hoses of *hookahs,* or water pipes, in between sips of the thick sweet coffee, which was served in tiny handleless cups.

But not all of Arabia's coffeehouses provided such sumptuous surroundings. A mid-eighteenth century European adventurer wrote home about his experiences upon reaching Yemen:

> On the first day of our journey, we rested in a coffeehouse near a village. Mokeya is the name given by the Arabs to such places as stand in open country. They are intended, like our inns, for the accommodation of travellers. They are mere huts and are scarcely furnished but with a long seat of straw ropes, nor do they afford any refreshment but a hot infusion of coffee beans. This drink is served out of coarse earthen cups, but personages of distinction carry fine porcelain cups in their baggage. The master of the coffeehouse commonly lives in a nearby village, from whence he comes every day to serve travellers.

Before long, coffeehouses turned into places of entertainment. Against a backdrop of music, men played chess and backgammon, and lively conversation was the rule. In some of the more adventuresome houses, singing and dancing became common.

Because alcohol is forbidden in Islamic societies, coffee is sometimes called "the wine of Islam." It warms and stimulates, but does not cloud the mind or cause drunkenness. Nonetheless, centuries ago, coffeehouses were once seen

Not just purveyors of coffee, but also centers of entertainment, early coffeehouses were a common site for chess games, storytelling, singing, and dancing.

as hotbeds of iniquity by devoutly religious Moslems. Coffee drinkers were reviled and coffeehouses were attacked by fanatics. From time to time, some rulers went so far as to ban coffee and decreed horrific punishments for those who drank "the devil's brew," but the furor always died down and the coffeehouses flourish still.

TURKEY

The first coffeehouse outside of Arabia was established in Constantinople in 1475. It was named Kiv Han, and immediately became a popular meeting place. By the early 1500s, Constantinople (Istanbul) boasted a total of three coffeehouses, establishments that were frequented by "beys, nobles, officers, teachers, judges and other people of the law." Like many of the coffeehouses of Arabia, those of Turkey's cities were often lavish affairs.

By the time of the sultanate of Murat IV (1623–1640), the coffeehouses of Constantinople had become meeting places of "mutinous soldiers" and those with grievances against authority. This worried the sultan and in 1633, Murat banned coffee and decreed that the coffeehouses be torn down. However, by the latter part of the 1600s, these popular establishments were once again open for business.

Turkey is famous for its coffee, which is much different from the brew enjoyed in Europe and the United States—although quite similar to the coffee enjoyed for centuries in Arabia. An old Turkish proverb says, "Coffee should be black as hell, as strong as death, and as sweet as love." When first poured, Turkish coffee is cloudy with the powdery grounds called *telve.* The cup is left to sit undisturbed for a minute or so to allow the telve to settle, forming a thick layer at the bottom of the cup. The clear coffee, about two inches of it, remains on top. (To learn more about how Turkish coffee is prepared, see page 99 of Chapter 6.)

In 1610, an adventuresome Englishman named George Sandys visited Constantinople. He wasn't much impressed by the thick, sweet drink so favored by the Turks. Here's a pertinent passage taken from his journal:

> Although the Turks be destitute of taverns, they have their coffa-houses, which somewhat resemble good English taverns. Many of the coffa proprietors send beautiful boys out in the streets to procure them customers. The men sit chatting most of the day and sip a drink called coffa in little china dishes as hot as they can suffer it—black as soot and tasting not much unlike it.

Despite the reaction of Sandys and other visitors from foreign lands, strong, sweet coffee has remained the favorite brew of the Turkish. And to this day, coffeehouses remain a place where family and friends gather both for refreshment and to discuss the topics of the day.

EGYPT

In the early 1500s, there were no coffeehouses in Egypt, but it didn't take long before Cairo was full of them. In 1530, a Turkish merchant wrote home:

> There is a concentration of coffeehouses at every step. Early rising worshippers and pious men get up and go there and drink a cup of coffee, adding life to their lives. They feel that the exhilaration strengthens them for their worship.

Earlier, you discovered that a number of the coffeehouses of Arabia and Turkey were quite lavish. The same was true of many Egyptian establishments. And in each of these houses, the same strong, sweet coffee was enjoyed.

Although some visitors to Turkey did not care for the country's strong, sweet coffee, others fell in love with all things Turkish. In seventeenth-century Paris, "Turkomania" took hold as fashionable people adopted both the dress and the exotic brew of the Turks.

For centuries, the love of coffee—and of coffeehouses—has crossed class lines. Sixteenth-century Egyptian governor Ahmet Pasa is perhaps best known for establishing coffeehouses for the needy, thereby insuring that both rich and poor could enjoy the coffeehouse experience.

On the other hand, many neighborhood Egyptian coffeehouses were nothing more than one small room outfitted with a few benches for patrons. On busy nights when a storyteller was spinning an exciting tale, customers perched anywhere they could find a seat, often on the stoop outside the establishment, or even on the steps of shops across the street. This type of coffeehouse was common not only in Egypt, but all across that part of the world, including Turkey and Syria.

Coffee crossed class lines both in Egypt and in other areas of the East. The beverage became so popular with the masses that in the latter part of the sixteenth century, Ahmet Pasa, the governor of Egypt, established coffeehouses for the needy. Strangely—or, perhaps, not so strangely, considering the Egyptians' devotion to coffee—although this leader funded many public works, he is best remembered for his largesse in bringing coffee to the poor. Today, both coffee and coffeehouses continue to play an important part in the lives of the Egyptian people.

ITALY

As discussed in Chapter 1, coffee arrived in Europe through the trading port of Venice and was an immediate sensation with nearly everyone. Predictably, though, it did have its small number of detractors. Soon after the new beverage's appearance, a Venetian writer by the name of Gianfrancesco Morosini penned a less-than-flattering picture of the coffee drinkers of the times:

All these people are quite base, of low costume and very little industry, such that for the most part they spend their time sunk in idleness. Thus they continually sit about, and for entertainment, they are in the habit of drinking, in public, in shops and in the streets—a black liquid, boiling as hot as they can stand it, which is extracted from a seed they call Cavee. It is said to have the property of keeping a man awake.

Finding far more admirers than critics, coffee soon became a much-beloved beverage in Italy. At first, coffee was dispensed by vendors, along with other drinks. But by the middle of the seventeenth century, the first coffeehouses had been established. Soon, coffeehouses such as the centuries-old Florians, which opened in Venice in 1720, became popular meeting places. By 1763, there were over 2,000 caffès in Italy. By the early 1980s, this number had grown to 200,000! Now, there seems to be a coffee bar or coffeehouse on every corner.

Many of the coffee bars in Italy are stand-up affairs. The customers stand at the bar, sipping and talking, bantering with the *baristas* (bartenders) who serve up fragrant steaming cupfuls. Some establishments offer both a bar and tables, but when ordered at a table, coffee costs several times as much as it does at a bar. It is interesting to note that in contrast to French cafés, where the pace is leisurely despite the increasingly hectic nature of French life, Italians tend to rush in and out of their coffee bars and caffès, downing their beverages in a minute or two.

Anyone who frequents coffeehouses in the United States is familiar with the beverages offered in Italian establishments. Espresso, caffè latte, and cappuccino were all born in Italy, and continue to be enjoyed there. Yet another common beverage found in Italy is caffè Americano—espresso brought to the equivalent of American drip coffee through dilution with hot water. (To learn about these and other common coffeehouse drinks, see page 111 of Chapter 7.)

Despite the early efforts of Roman priests to have coffee drinking prohibited among Christians, the first Italian coffeehouse opened in 1645.

ENGLAND

The first coffeehouse in London opened its doors in 1652. But perhaps a better-known coffeehouse appeared in 1687, when it was established in London by Edward Loyd. From the outset, Loyd's was popular with merchants and wealthy ship owners. Not surprisingly, maritime insurance agents also began frequenting Loyd's establishment. Spacious and comfortable, the coffeehouse

Lloyd's of London, the world-famous insurance firm, began as a coffeehouse that catered mostly to merchants and seafarers—and, not surprisingly, to under-writers who sold maritime insurance to the coffeehouse's loyal patrons.

was a pleasant place to do business. So many insurance contracts were negoti-ated at Loyd's heavy mahogany tables that eventually the coffeehouse gave way to Lloyd's of London, the insurance company. (Somewhere along the way, the company's name acquired an extra "l.")

By 1675, every English city, township, and village boasted several coffee-houses. This was when King Charles II decided to outlaw such establishments. His advisors convinced him that the very foundation of the English family was trembling because men were neglecting their families, preferring instead to spend idle hours discussing business and politics over coffee. The public out-cry against the ill-advised proclamation was so universal that the decree was revoked.

By 1715, as many as 2,000 coffeehouses had sprung up in London alone. Although open to every class, houses did tend to develop reputations based on clientele. Some, for instance, distinctly drew businessmen. In fact, prior to the establishment of the London Stock Exchange in 1773, all the buying and selling was conducted by brokers in one of the many coffeehouses in the city.

Incidentally, the custom of tipping was born in an English coffeehouse, presumably in the seventeenth century. A strategically placed cup was backed by a sign reading: "To Insure Prompt Service." Patrons were expected to drop in some coins if they wanted fast service and a seat at one of the better tables. The idea caught on. Soon every establishment had cups at the ready. TIPS, the abbreviation of the phrase, entered the lexicon, and tipping was here to stay.

From the beginning, most English coffeehouses served alcohol, chocolate, and tea as well as coffee, which was prepared much as American coffee is today. As you probably know, tea eventually overtook coffee in popularity, and even today remains the beverage of choice throughout the British Isles. Although coffee bars became popular again in the 1950s, for many years, the English sometimes seemed almost indifferent to the delights of the many forms of the brew that were common elsewhere. However, the late 1990s saw a renewed interest in a good cup of coffee on the part of many Brits, and coffee bars and houses began again popping up everywhere, with lattes and cappuccinos gaining favor.

FRANCE

For centuries, tea was the preferred beverage in France. But beginning in the late 1600s, coffee gradually became the drink of choice.

The first French coffeehouse was established in Paris in 1672. The proprietor was a Paris-based Armenian merchant named Pascal who had enjoyed success selling coffee to the public from a stall set up at the fair of St. Germaine. This was the first time coffee was offered to all comers, rather than just the upper echelons of society. Encouraged by the enthusiasm of the fair-goers, Pascal promptly opened a small shop on the Quai de l'Evole, where he is said to have made a comfortable living. Another café, Le Procope, opened in Paris in 1686. By 1800, Paris boasted close to 3,000 coffeehouses.

Today, the sidewalk cafés of France are legendary. Natives and tourists alike often start the day with a large cup of café au lait, strong coffee gentled with hot milk; recharge in the afternoon with a cappuccino—espresso topped with steamed milk; and pause after dinner for a black coffee accompanied by brandy. In France, coffee is far more than a mere beverage. It is a way of life.

AUSTRIA

Austria's first coffeehouse was opened in Vienna in 1683 by Franz Georg Kolschitzky. According to legend, Kolschitzky's venture was one of the results of the 1683 Siege of Vienna. Here's the story.

From 1663 through 1664, Austria was at war with the Turks. Although this war ended in victory for the Austrians, some nobles from neighboring Hun-

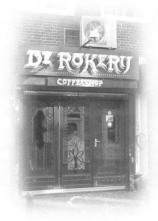

Not everyone was pleased by the growth of coffeehouses. In seventeenth-century England, tavern owners, worried by the loss of business, condemned coffee as an evil drink; and women, whose husbands spent more time in coffeehouses than at home, printed "The Women's Petition Against Coffee."

gary were unhappy with the outcome and began conspiring against the Habsburgs, hereditary rulers of Austria. The nobles were joined by Austrian rebels, known as the Kuruzen (Crusaders), and in 1679, by the fierce Turks. By 1683, the Turkish army had surrounded Vienna and things were looking pretty bleak for the Austrians. Kolschitzky, our hero, managed to slip through enemy lines and bring relief forces to the beleaguered city.

As the cavalry rode to the rescue, the Turks rode out in haste, leaving behind what was described as "dry, black fodder." It was Kolschitzky who recognized that the "fodder" was actually coffee and who claimed the sacks of coffee, which no one else wanted. When the city had settled down, he opened a coffeehouse. Several sources say that it was Kolschitzky who first began the practice of filtering out the coffee grounds from the brew. He is also credited with adding sweetener and milk.

By the 1700s, all of Austria was drinking coffee, and in Vienna, the coffeehouse became an institution—and has remained one for over three centuries. Almost a second living room, the coffeehouse is used by the Austrians not only as a place to drink their favorite beverage and eat their pastries, but also as a comfortable haven in which to play cards, read, and chat with friends.

The Viennese like their coffee served with a drift of whipped cream crowning the cup. Additions such as brandy are also popular.

GERMANY

Germans had become aware of coffee through travels in the Middle East in the latter part of the 1500s. But, partly because of ongoing prohibitions and taxes, it wasn't until the late 1700s that coffee became a popular beverage in the German home. Interestingly, though, the first coffeehouse opened in Hamburg far earlier—around 1680—and soon after, coffeehouses cropped up throughout the country.

In 1732, composer Johann Sebastian Bach acknowledged Germany's growing love of coffee with his *Kafee-Kantate,* or *Coffee Cantata.* This composition is often described as a paean to coffee's pleasures, but was actually Bach's sly ridicule of a movement afoot in Germany to prevent women from drinking coffee on the grounds that it could make them sterile. The cantata includes the words, "Ah! How sweet coffee tastes! Lovelier than a thousand kisses; sweeter far than muscatel wine! I must have coffee!"

By 1900, German hausfraus had established a pleasant custom of their own. Because they weren't welcome in public coffeehouses, the ladies gathered together in small groups at one another's houses to sip coffee and talk. A mid-afternoon gathering of women thus came to be known as a *kaffeklatsch*—a combination of *kaffe,* the term for coffee, and *klatsch,* or gossip.

Once the coffee habit had become firmly entrenched in German culture, no government bans—and no prohibitions against women in coffeehouses—could destroy Germany's love of the beverage. In fact, today, coffee consumption is higher in Germany than it is anywhere else in Europe, and coffeehouses, called coffee bars, offer the same beverages found in Italy and France.

When they failed to receive a welcome in local coffeehouses, German housewives met at one another's homes for coffee (*kaffe*) and gossip (*klatsch*). And the *kaffeklatsch* was born.

NORTH AMERICA

As you learned in Chapter 1, coffee may have travelled to Colonial America with Captain John Smith in the early 1600s. But it was decades before the first coffeehouse appeared in the colonies, and centuries before coffeehouses became a common stop in the daily lives of so many people throughout the United States and Canada.

Early American Coffeehouses

The first coffeehouse in North America was established in St. Mary's City,

Like their European counterparts, early American coffeehouses were often the center for political, social, and business interactions. Boston's Green Dragon coffeehouse played an important role in the American Revolution, while plans for the Bank of New York were finalized at the Merchant's Coffee House.

Maryland in the late 1600s by a Dutchman named Garrit Van Swearingen. Van Swearingen first opened a popular inn, where, it is said, members of the General Assembly held meetings. Although the exact date is not recorded, surviving records show that Van Swearingen eventually opened a coffeehouse in a small outbuilding adjacent to the inn. Artifacts, including the remnants of several coffee services, have been unearthed at the site. By all accounts, Van Swearingen's coffeehouse was very popular in its day.

Boston got its first coffeehouse in 1670. The establishment was unusual in that its owner was a woman named Dorothy Jones. Better known, however, is the Green Dragon, which opened its doors on Boston's Union Street in 1697. Early on, this coffeehouse became a meeting place for British redcoats, officers of the crown, and leading citizens. As time went on, the house functioned as an unofficial town hall where citizens had their say and hotly argued politics. It is believed that the idea for the Boston Tea Party—widely recognized as the beginning of the end of British rule—was born at this coffeehouse in 1773. Indeed, Daniel Webster named the Green Dragon "the headquarters of the revolution."

Just as Loyd's coffeehouse eventually evolved into Lloyd's of London, the Bank of New York began in a coffeehouse. The plans for the founding of the Bank of New York—the city's first financial institution—were first formulated and then finalized at the Merchant's Coffee House in New York City in 1784. Indeed, just like many European cities, American cities were quick to use their coffeehouses as centers for business transactions, as well as social and political interactions. Although a good many financial dealings were carried out under a tree at 68 Wall Street, New York's Tontine Coffee House did double duty as a comfortable place in which to buy and sell stocks. Trading at the Tontine continued until the New York Stock and Exchange Board was established in 1817.

By all accounts, the Tontine was a most spacious, handsomely furnished, and very elegantly appointed establishment. It was not only a center for financial wheeling and dealing, but was also favored as "the" place to hold a ball or a banquet or to entertain clients and important visitors. In fact, the Tontine was so well known for its magnificence that, in its day, it was one of the most famous sights in the city.

The Coffeehouse Tradition Changes

After the mid-1800s, special spots like the Tontine all but disappeared for a long time. From the 1940s to the mid-1950s, small coffee shops and diners were popular meeting and dining spots, but these establishments placed a greater focus on hot turkey sandwiches and meatloaf than on coffee, which was viewed just as "a cup of Joe."

The Bohemian coffeehouses of the late 1950s and 1960s sprang up in the days of hot coffee, cool jazz, raw poetry, and readings designed to shock. Nevertheless, Jack Kerouac and other members of the Beat Generation were more often found in bars than in coffeehouses.

In the middle of the 1960s, the hippies of San Francisco's Haight-Ashbury district made coffeehouses the place to hang out, hear folk music and poetry, or listen to some up-and-coming comedians. The movement spread across the United States, and soon just about every community had an enclave of "flower children." The coffee hadn't improved much, but nobody cared because the focus was most definitely not on food.

Several experts have traced the decline of the coffeehouses of the period to the birth of rock 'n' roll. While jazz and folk music were ideally suited to the intimate and relaxed atmosphere of a coffeehouse, the hard-driving rhythm of rock 'n' roll was more appreciated in a concert setting. In the meantime, most Americans were still drinking their coffee at home or in coffee shops and restaurants.

During the mid-sixties, the popularity of both coffee and coffeehouses began to decline throughout the United States. But when specialty coffees appeared on the market in the eighties, Americans resumed their love affair with the coffee bean.

The Rebirth of the Coffeehouse

As you've seen, during several decades of the 1900s, the coffeehouse was largely a neglected institution in America. But late in the mid-1980s, everything changed when the appearance of specialty coffees breathed new life into

Starbucks—America's Coffeehouse

As most Americans know, Starbucks Coffee Company has had a great deal to do with the phenomenal growth of coffeehouses throughout the United States. What many Americans do not know is that the story of Starbucks Coffee actually began half a century ago with a Dutchman by the name of Alfred Peet.

Alfred Peet, a Dutch tea and coffee trader with an appreciation for fine tea and coffee and the ability to tell the difference between mediocre and marvelous, moved to California in the 1950s. Unable to stomach the pale robusta brews that Americans were drinking at that time, Peet imported high-quality arabica beans from the far corners of the world. In 1966, he opened Peet's Coffee and Tea in Berkeley, where he sold whole beans. He did his own roasting, always matching the roast to the bean, and favored dark roasts. It took awhile, but Americans eventually began mail-ordering their coffee from Peet. That success encouraged other coffee aficionados, and a few specialty roasters began opening shops in other areas of the country.

Among Peet's early converts were Jerry Baldwin, Gordon Bowker, and Zev Siegl, the founders of Starbucks. The first Starbucks coffee store the coffeehouse. Suddenly, espresso—previously, an "exotic" drink found only in Italian restaurants and Bohemian hideaways—was available in coffeehouses across the country, along with a variety of other specialty coffee drinks. Before the coffeehouse explosion, fewer than 500 such establishments could be found

opened in Seattle, Washington in 1971. In those early days, Starbucks didn't routinely sell coffee by the cup, although it sometimes offered a taste of the roast of the day. What the company did give its customers was a selection of the finest coffee beans from around the world. Just like Peet, Starbucks roasted in-house to insure that the quality was consistent.

It was Howard Schultz—the man who would ultimately take over the company—who presided over the opening of the first Starbucks to offer specialty coffees by the cup, as well as selling whole beans. His dream was to recreate the coffee bar experience he had discovered and loved in Italy. The experiment was wildly successful. Customers were delighted with the unfamiliar espresso, cappuccino, and caffè latte that Schultz's baristas expertly prepared and served. Everything clicked. Before very long, the coffee bar was generating even more income than the sale of beans.

In 1987, the original owners of Starbucks sold the company to Howard Schultz, and expansion was the name of the game. The history of the wild ride that culminated in the appearance of a Starbucks in every community in the nation is chronicled in Howard Schultz's book, Pour Your Heart Into It.

With more than 3,000 thriving Starbucks outlets in North America alone, Starbucks' story is definitely one of success. Part of the company's secret is its quest for the highest-quality coffee beans and the variety it offers in the form of hot and cold beverages and pastries. But a portion of its success is due to the pleasures offered by the coffeehouse experience itself—an experience that has entranced coffee drinkers worldwide for hundreds of years.

nationwide. By the close of the twentieth century, the number had grown to 10,000.

To many Americans, the word "coffeehouse" brings the Starbucks Coffee chain to mind. (For information on the Starbucks phenomenon, see the inset on pages 54 to 55.) But Starbucks isn't the only specialty roaster in North America. A number of companies—Tully's, Peet's, and Gloria Jean's Coffee Bean, for instance—now offer prepared coffee and coffee drinks, as well as whole beans, of course. Some coffeehouses are outfitted with tables and chairs, both inside and outside. Some are formal, but most are relaxed. For many people, the coffeehouse is once again the place to go at night and just hang out. People drift in and out, joining one group or another, and there are stimulating discussions of everything under the sun. A poetry reading or evening of music always draws a crowd. Open-mike nights, where anyone who wishes can perform, are usually well attended.

A recent coffee house phenomenon—not just in the United States, but all over the world—is the *cybercafe*, where banks of computers with Internet access are available for an hour or two for a small fee. Customers send and receive e-mail, keep up with local news, or dig out information from the web. For those unfamiliar with the intricacies of cyberspace, help is usually close at hand. And, of course, like all coffeehouses, cybercafes offer a range of beverages, both plain and fancy.

Although its popularity has waxed and waned over the years, it's clear that the coffeehouse is here to stay. The lure of companionship is certainly part of the draw. And so is the enticing taste and smell of the coffee itself. But, as you will learn in the next chapter, people crave coffee for more than just its flavor. Many credit it with health benefits—its ability to combat fatigue and to relieve headache, for instance. Just how helpful (or harmful) is this beverage? Chapter 4 explores the subject of coffee and your health.

Coffee and Your Health

*Coffee quickens the mind
and lets the spirit fly.*

—CHARLES MONTAGU,
EARL OF HALIFAX (1661–1715)

When the coffee bean made its way to Europe from Arabia, it was viewed as welcome medicine by the medicos of the day. Since then, coffee has received both positive and negative reviews from health professionals. The good news is that this much-adored beverage now is not only known to be perfectly safe for the vast majority of coffee lovers, but, after decades of research, is recognized as providing some important health benefits. This chapter examines how coffee was viewed by the health community in the past and discusses what we now know about the coffee bean and your health.

A HISTORICAL OVERVIEW

One reason for England's initial embrace of coffee was the belief that coffee was an antidote to drunkenness. To the relief of doctors everywhere, many people began to choose the "wakeful and civil drink" of coffee over ale, beer, and wine.

Coffee had been enjoyed and revered in the East for years when it appeared on the scene in Europe. Immediately, people had strong opinions about the substance's good or ill effects. Interestingly, the view of coffee was partly determined by the view of another popular beverage—alcohol.

In the 1600s, melancholia (depression) was a widespread problem in England, and doctors were desperately seeking a cure. Misery and poverty were contributing factors, but by far the greatest cause of this affliction was acknowledged to be chronic alcoholism. Robert Burton (1577–1640), the Anglican clergyman who wrote *The Anatomy of Melancholy* in 1621 and is recognized as a keen observer of the life and times of his contemporaries, wrote, "Many men, knowing that merry company is the only medicine against melancholy, will spend all their days among good fellows in a tavern in drinking, seeth their brains in ale, contract filthy diseases, heat their livers, spoil their stomachs, and overthrow their bodies for drink."

The physicians of the time were seeking an antidote to drunkenness, as well as to a number of health problems related to excessive alcohol consumption. Burton suggested that coffee might be the cure that all were seeking. He understood that coffee sobers men, and wrote, "The Turks find by experience, that kind of drink, so used, helpeth digestion and procureth alacrity."

Some of the best minds of the times decided that the "coffee drug" was worth trying. One of the first to secure a supply of coffee beans from Arabia was Dr. William Harvey (1578–1657), who is known for discovering how blood circulates throughout the body. In his dispensary, Harvey labeled it *Coff. Arab.*, and shared the results of his careful experiments with his colleagues.

One of Harvey's pupils, Edward Pococke, took Harvey's results and amplified them outrageously. Pococke not only recommended coffee as a cure for drunkenness, as did Harvey, but wrote that, "Taken [after] fasting, the first thing in the morning, it is of the utmost value in consumption, ophthalmia, and dropsy and will cure gout and scurvy and even prevent smallpox." In the end, these overenthusiastic endorsements caused many to disregard the very real beneficial effects of coffee. The one thing that all those testing coffee agreed upon was that it was able "to cure drunkards." Broadsides (flyers) given out to passersby on the street took opposing positions. Here are brief excerpts from two mid-seventeenth century flyers—one pro and one con.

> Do but this Rare Arabian Cordial use
> and thou may'st all the Doctor's Slops Refuse.

> Syrop of soot and Essence of Old Shoes
> A loathsome Potion not yet understood.

When Dr. Harvey died in 1657, coffee was being widely prescribed by doctors, and Europe's coffeehouses were gaining in popularity. In his will, Harvey bequeathed a fifty-six-pound bag of the best coffee berries to the London College of Physicians. He asked that his colleagues meet monthly, brew a potful, and drink to his memory.

It was true that coffee was not yet understood. Some doctors regarded the beverage as a useful drug; others were openly skeptical. Most were of two minds. One, a Dr. Willis, warned against the excessive drinking of coffee, but admitted privately that he sometimes sent his patients to a coffeehouse instead of the apothecary.

Across the channel in France, the controversy over coffee's effects on the body were also being debated—and would be for another century at least. It's been reported that François Marie Arouet de Voltaire (1694–1778), the tart-tongued writer and philosopher who was a leading figure of the eighteenth

Throughout the 1600s and 1700s, Europeans attributed many healing properties to coffee. Some doctors even regarded it as a remedy to the plague!

century, drank fifty cups of coffee a day. Near the end of his life, Voltaire wrote, "If coffee be poison, I have been poisoning myself for more than eighty years and I am not yet dead." Voltaire called coffee "an exceedingly cerebral liquor"—a fact that has since been proven true by scientific research.

Whether people have condemned coffee or recommended it, over the ages, everyone seems to have agreed that coffee has a marked effect on the body. Let's examine why and how coffee affects us.

WHAT'S IN COFFEE?

From a nutritional point of view, a cup of coffee provides about 0.5 gram of carbohydrate, a tiny 0.01 gram of fat, and only 3 calories. In addition, your morning cupful includes 1.26 milligrams of niacin and 117 milligrams of potassium, plus the merest traces of vitamin B_2, copper, iron, magnesium, manganese, phosphorus, sodium, and zinc.

Obviously, coffee is no nutritional powerhouse. Yet, as mentioned earlier, coffee has noticeable effects on the body, the most obvious of which is its ability to stimulate. What's in the cup that gives this beverage its delightful stimulating qualities? The caffeine, of course. In fact, caffeine seems to be responsible for most of coffee's effects. In addition, coffee contains a diverse array of compounds with antioxidant properties.

Caffeine

Although coffee contains hundreds of chemicals, its main active ingredient is caffeine—the substance responsible for coffee's ability to boost alertness and mood.

Caffeine is a naturally occurring alkaloid that is found in the coffee plant, as well as in more than sixty other plants found worldwide. It is odorless, but it has a bitter taste.

After coffee is consumed, a gentle jolt can be felt as its stimulating effects come into play. Even a small amount of caffeine "wakes up" the brain cells,

Even Then, They Knew

In the last few decades, scientific research has indicated why coffee has specific effects on the body. (To read about some of this research, turn to page 64.) But hundreds of years ago—long before modern science analyzed the various components of coffee—herbalists recognized the unique effects of the coffee bean and recommended it for the treatment of various ailments. Here are just a few of the conditions for which traditional practitioners have prescribed coffee:

Heart problems. Hundreds of years ago, herbalists identified coffee as an active brain and heart stimulant. As an aid to a flagging heart, practicing herbalists often recommended that coffee be taken with foxglove tea, which is the source of digitalis, a known cardiac stimulant.

Poisoning. Coffee has been used for centuries to counteract narcotic poisonings. In addition, it was once considered valuable in cases of snakebite because it was believed to prevent the patient from lapsing into a dangerous coma.

Headache. Herbalists noted long ago that a migraine or other type of throbbing headache can be eased by taking one or two cups of strong coffee.

Asthma. Herbalists have long known that a cup of coffee can sometimes stop an asthma attack and restore clear breathing.

which helps reduce feelings of drowsiness, weariness, and fatigue. In addition, the heart responds to caffeine by beating a bit faster, which causes the blood to circulate with greater speed. For a short time, blood pressure may also increase. That's why some doctors advise patients with low blood pressure to drink a cup of caffeinated coffee in the morning upon rising.

In the stomach, small amounts of caffeine act to increase the production of stomach acids, which, in turn, help the digestive process. The kidneys react to caffeine by increasing the production of urine, which makes it an effective diuretic.

Researchers have also found that caffeine has the ability to boost the effectiveness of certain other drugs. Pharmacists call caffeine a *potentiator*, which means that it increases the effects of the substance with which it's mated. For this reason, you'll find caffeine in some weight-control pills, diuretics, stimulants, pain relievers, and cold and allergy remedies. Because of its stimulating effects, caffeine is also used to counteract the drowsiness that certain drugs cause. Be aware, however, that caffeine is known to interfere with the actions of some prescription drugs.

Are all the effects of caffeine good? Well, no. Adverse symptoms caused by too much caffeine include rapid heartbeat, excessive urination, stomach and bowel distress, restlessness, and insomnia. Excessive caffeine consumption can also cause vitamins and minerals, including iron, to be excreted by the body before they are utilized.

Depending on the roast and how it was brewed, an eight-ounce cup of coffee (regular, not decaffeinated) contains 65 to 120 milligrams of caffeine. (Turn to the inset on page 63 to see how the caffeine content of coffee measures up to that of other beverages.) Strong coffee can contain as much as 200 milligrams in six ounces.

It is a documented fact that caffeine works fast. About five minutes after you drink your morning coffee, caffeine is present in the tissues of the body and the brain. It reaches peak blood levels in twenty to thirty minutes, and then begins to decline. After three to six hours, about half the caffeine has been used up. After another three to six hours, only a quarter of the caffeine is still present. Only one percent of caffeine is not metabolized. That tiny bit is excreted naturally.

How much caffeine is too much? You are your own best judge. If you have trouble sleeping after a cup of after-dinner coffee, next time, make it decaf. If several cups of coffee make you feel jittery and nervous, back off. If you find yourself relying on cup after cup of strong coffee to keep you going through-

Although espresso has a higher concentration of caffeine than regular coffee, the average serving is far smaller—only one to two ounces. Therefore, the caffeine content of an espresso is comparable to that of a standard cup of Joe.

The Caffeine Count

By far, the major source of caffeine in the American diet is coffee. However, coffee is not the only dietary source of caffeine. As you learned earlier in the chapter, caffeine is present in over sixty plants found throughout the world, including tea leaves, cocoa beans, and the kola nut. That's why caffeine is also found in tea, chocolate, and colas.

The following table provides a look at the average amount of caffeine found in different beverages, including several different types of coffee. Keep in mind, though, that in coffee, variations in caffeine content can be caused by many factors, including the variety of coffee bean, the kind of roast, the particular coffee grind, and the length of brewing time.

THE CAFFEINE CONTENT OF COMMON BEVERAGES

Type of Coffee	Caffeine Content
Brewed (8-ounce cup)	65–120 mg
Instant (8-ounce cup)	65–85 mg
Decaffeinated, brewed (8-ounce cup)	2–4 mg
Decaffeinated, instant (8-ounce cup)	1–4 mg
Espresso (1-ounce cup)	30–50 mg

Other Beverages	Caffeine Content
Tea (8-ounce cup)	22–36 mg
Hot Chocolate (5-ounce cup)	2–20 mg
Colas (12-ounce can)	41–46 mg

out a long day and into the night when working on some project, beware. Authorities say that a heavy intake of caffeine—such as the 1,000 milligrams contained in five to ten cups of coffee, depending on the strength of the brew—can cause nasty symptoms, including a feeling of restlessness, trembling of the limbs, insomnia, diarrhea, and even heart palpitations. But unless you have a sensitivity to caffeine, you can easily drink up to three cups of coffee per day and enjoy its beneficial effects, such as pleasant stimulation, increased mental acuity, and lessened fatigue.

Antioxidants

A little-known fact is that coffee contains *four times* the antioxidants found in green tea. Some of these health-enhancing substances are thought to be created during the roasting process.

Toward the end of the twentieth century, scientists began discovering the power of *antioxidants*—organic substances that are thought to be effective in helping prevent cancer, heart disease, and other disorders. Antioxidants protect the body by destroying *free radicals*—substances that can damage cell structures, thereby leading to disease. Free radicals are the byproducts of many processes within the body, and can also be created by exposure to environmental factors such as tobacco smoke.

You may have heard that green tea is rich in antioxidants, and therefore is a valuable health-enhancing beverage. But research has shown that coffee contains *four times* the antioxidants found in green tea. Coffee expert Takayuki Shibamoto, professor of environmental toxicology at the University of California, says that if coffee is consumed within twenty minutes of brewing, you receive the benefit of 300 *phytochemicals*—naturally occurring substances with antioxidant properties—for up to thirty days. In addition to the antioxidants found in the raw beans, substances with antioxidant activity are thought to be generated during the roasting process. Although the research on antioxidants in coffee is still in its infancy, further study is sure to reveal additional benefits of coffee.

HOW DOES COFFEE AFFECT YOUR HEALTH?

You now are familiar with the activity of caffeine, a major biologically active substance in coffee. And you have read—possibly for the first time—about how coffee is now known to contain antioxidants. Yet in the past, it is likely that you heard reports of the beverage's ill effects. Perhaps you read that coffee contains potential cancer-causing substances, or that it contributes to heart disease. Because caffeinated foods and beverages are so commonplace in the Western diet, the health effects of coffee and caffeine have been studied for years. During the 1970s and 1980s, research findings appeared to be contradictory, and some, like the ones just mentioned, were quite frightening. In more recent years, however, research has demonstrated not only that moderate coffee drinking is safe, but also that it can have some true health benefits. Let's see exactly what science has to say about the relationship between coffee and your health.

Coffee and Cancer

Earlier in the chapter, you learned that coffee contains antioxidants—substances that can help protect against a variety of disorders, including cancer. Scientists at Rutgers University have discovered that one such antioxidant, *caffeic acid*, prevents the body from converting sodium nitrite and sodium nitrate into nasty nitrosamines, which are known cancer-causing agents. Nitrites and nitrates are used in curing many meats, including bacon and salami. It's been known for some time that the antioxidant vitamins C and E can stop the conversion process. In fact, many cured meat producers add vitamin C to their products to cancel the harmful effects of nitrites and nitrates. The surprise was that caffeic acid not only accomplishes the same thing, but does it more efficiently.

The best news of all is that studies conducted at the University of British Colombia took it all one step further. Research scientists there determined that these effects can occur outside the laboratory as well. They discovered that it doesn't take pure caffeic acid to do the job. Coffee—brewed, instant, and even decaffeinated—also blocks the conversion process. Better yet, it does so in amounts ordinarily consumed by ordinary people.

Other studies, too, have indicated that coffee has cancer-fighting effects. An analysis of seventeen studies on coffee consumption and colorectal cancer found the risk of colorectal cancer to be 24-percent lower among people who drink four or more cups of coffee a day than it is among those who rarely or

Coffee consumption does not appear to increase the risk of any form of cancer, and significantly *decreases* the risk of colorectal cancer.

never drink coffee. The mechanism through which coffee helps prevent these cancers has not been proven. However, some researchers have suggested that frequent coffee drinking may decrease the excretion of bile acids, which are suspected to be carcinogenic to the colon. The antioxidants found in coffee may also play a role.

Coffee and Cardiovascular Disease

Years ago, some studies indicated that coffee was linked to an increase in serum cholesterol levels and an associated increased risk of heart disease. For many coffee lovers, these studies were a cause for concern—as well as confusion when different research findings appeared to be contradictory. The good news is that since then, other studies have shown *no* association between coffee intake and any type of cardiovascular disease. Surprised? Let's take a look at some of the results.

A controlled study of 340 men and woman with no prior history of heart disease was conducted at Brigham & Women's Hospital by Dr. Howard D. Sesso of Harvard Medical School and colleagues. The results, published in a 1999 paper entitled "Coffee and Tea Intake and the Risk of Myocardial Infarction," showed that coffee has no impact on the risk of heart attack. The outcome was the same whether the coffee was caffeinated or decaffeinated, and applied even to those coffee lovers who drank more than four cups daily.

These findings confirmed the results of several other long-term studies. For example, a ten-year study of more than 85,000 women, published in 1996, concluded that women are not at increased risk of cardiovascular disease even when consuming up to six cups of coffee daily. In 1990, the coffee-drinking habits of more than 45,000 men were studied. This study concluded that even in men drinking four or more cups of coffee a day, there is no link between coffee intake and heart disease.

You may have heard of the Framingham Heart Study, an ongoing study that has followed more than 6,000 adult men and women to investigate factors that may have an impact on heart health. This study has reached the same conclusion as the others: Whether caffeinated or decaffeinated, there is no discernible link between coffee and heart disease. Period.

Before we leave the subject of cardiovascular disease, it's important to return to an earlier section of the chapter, where you learned that caffeine can raise blood pressure. This might lead you to conclude that coffee consumption can contribute to *hypertension,* or high blood pressure. However, studies have indicated that while first-time caffeine use may produce immediate, though minimal, changes in blood pressure, no changes in blood pressure appear to occur in people who drink coffee on a regular basis.

Coffee and Stone Formation

Researchers have conducted several studies investigating the relationship between coffee drinking and the formation of kidney stones and gallstones. The results? Coffee has been found to actually *reduce* the risk of stone formation.

One study looked at 45,000 men with no history of kidney stones. Researchers found that greater intakes of both regular and decaffeinated coffee—as well as tea, beer, and wine—are associated with a decreased risk of kidney stone formation. A further study involving 81,000 women showed that caffeinated coffee and wine are significantly more effective in helping women avoid kidney stones than is water, which is generally thought to have stone-protective properties. Specifically, an eight-ounce serving of coffee appears to lower risk by about 10 percent.

Research on gallstone disease has shown even more dramatic results. A ten-year study of men concluded that the consumption of two to three cups of regular (caffeinated) coffee per day lowers the risk of developing gallstones by

Although patients with kidney stones are routinely advised to increase their intake of water, research has indicated that coffee has far more powerful stone-fighting effects.

40 percent. And when men increase their intake to four or more cups a day, the risk is decreased by as much as 45 percent.

Coffee, Alertness, and Mood

Coffee lovers everywhere rely on their wake-up cup to clear away the cobwebs and prepare them for the day. And research has confirmed that coffee improves not only alertness but also mood.

In 1993, a study was conducted to examine the effects of coffee on daytime and nighttime performance and alertness. The results demonstrated that regular coffee consumption improves both alertness and performance in a variety of tasks during both the day and the night. Other studies have established that a cup of regular coffee after lunch can help counteract the normal "post-lunch dip" and allow workers to maintain concentration and productivity. And, according to two studies, coffee—when coupled with a thirty-minute break— can help prevent the road accidents caused by driver sleepiness. In fact, studies have indicated that even people who are not fatigued show enhanced performance, including improved athletic performance, as well as greater alertness and efficiency as the result of coffee consumption.

In addition to boosting alertness, coffee appears to enhance mood. Coffee consumption seems to decrease the risk of suicide, reduce irritability, and increase self-confidence and social skills. Coffee has been shown to help lift depression—even chronic depression. Coffee drinkers are also less likely to use anti-anxiety and anti-psychotic medications.

Coffee and Asthma

For a long time, anecdotal evidence has shown that regular coffee consumption can moderate asthma attacks. Science has supported this with two large studies, both of which concluded that three or more cups of coffee a day can reduce the prevalence of asthma symptoms by relaxing bronchial muscles, and thereby widening air passages in the lungs. However, doctors warn that care must be taken to avoid excessive coffee drinking, which can cause overstimulation in susceptible individuals.

Coffee and Women's Health

For years, there has been much concern over the relationship between coffee, caffeine, and women's health. A number of aspects have been considered, including reproductive health, osteoporosis, and breast disease. Let's look at the findings.

Many researchers have questioned whether coffee drinking is safe for pregnant women. Today, most physicians and researchers agree that it is. Daily consumption of two to three cups of brewed coffee a day appears to have no adverse reproductive consequences. It has been suggested, however, that women who wish to be cautious should limit their coffee consumption to two cups per day.

Can coffee delay or decrease fertility in women who are planning to become pregnant? Again, studies indicate that coffee has no adverse effects on the reproductive process. Therefore, women who wish to become pregnant need not eliminate coffee or other sources of caffeine from their diet—although moderation is always wise.

Many researchers have investigated the possible effects of coffee drinking on *osteoporosis,* a disease that can lead to weak and brittle bones. Fortunately, a number of well-controlled studies have concluded that moderate amounts of caffeine do not increase a woman's risk of developing this problem. Instead, researchers emphasize the importance of women building adequate bone mass during their teenage years.

Although studies in the 1970s and 1980s were contradictory, later research confirmed that moderate caffeine consumption poses no threat to women's health.

At one time, you may have read about an early study of women with *fibro-cystic breast disease* (FBD), a condition characterized by multiple cysts that can be felt throughout the breast. That study concluded that caffeine adds to the risk of developing FBD. However, later studies, including a study of 3,400 women conducted by the National Cancer Institute, found no association between caffeine intake and FBD. Like all other research investigating the relationship between coffee drinking and women's health, this study found that women can enjoy coffee without compromising their well-being.

See? Coffee isn't the "guilty pleasure" you may have thought. In fact, there's no reason why you can't have a cup of your favorite coffee right now—and there are some excellent reasons why you should. If you don't have a favorite, the next chapter will steer you in the right direction. That's where you'll learn all about the coffees of the world, from the well-known Colombian coffee to some mighty rare beans, plus everything else in between. I call it going from the sublime (Colombian) to the ridiculous (you'll see). Keep reading.

CHAPTER 5

Coffees of the World

*After all these years, the United States remains captivated by Colombia—
by the power of Colombian art, the force of Colombian literature, and, I might
add, the strength of Colombian coffee. Indeed, if ever a prize is given to any
of the people who negotiated the peace treaty at Wye, something will have to
be given to Colombia, for without the coffee, it would not have occurred.*

—PRESIDENT WILLIAM JEFFERSON CLINTON, OCTOBER 1998

The quotation that opens this chapter was taken from the speech President Clinton delivered in welcoming Colombian President Andres Pastrana to a State Dinner at the White House. The President's remarks acknowledged the part that Colombian coffee played in keeping the Israelis, Arabs, and Americans awake during the Wye Summit.

As you'll learn in this chapter, Colombian coffee has won kudos for its superior quality. But nowadays, coffee beans come to us from many different lands, giving us a wide selection of coffees from which we can choose. This chapter first looks at how coffee is rated, so that you'll understand who decides, for instance, that one bean is "winey" and another is not. The chapter then discusses many of the more readily available coffees grown around the world today.

RATING THE BEANS

A professional sampling of coffees to insure quality—a process referred to as *cupping*—occurs several times after coffee is harvested, both in the country that produces the coffee and in the country that buys it. For each cupping, a small batch of beans is roasted and ground. But interestingly, the ground coffee is not then brewed to provide a sample beverage. Instead, a small amount of the grounds is placed in a cup, and hot, not boiling, water is poured over the grounds, which float to the top of the cup and form a "crust." The taster, or cupper, then breaks the crust with the stir of a spoon, inhales the aroma, and finally "slurps" the liquid. Slurping, rather than polite sipping, is important, as it mixes oxygen with the coffee, bringing out the flavors. Each sample is tasted twice in quick succession.

Tasters judge beans primarily on flavor, acidity, and body. *Flavor* refers to how coffee tastes, as well as how it smells. For example, a good coffee may be judged "winey," with a whiff of chocolate in its aroma. Coffee described as "earthy" is considered less desirable. *Acidity* refers to a taste sensation that is created as the acids in the coffee combine with the sugars. Coffees that lack acidity are considered flat and dull. *Body* refers to how the coffee feels in the mouth. The coffee may be rated from "thin" to "syrupy," and anywhere in between. (To learn some basic coffee tasting terminology, see the inset on pages 79 and 80.)

Coffee tasting is performed "blind" so that the tasters have no idea what coffee they are rating. This is a highly specialized profession. Cuppers are akin to wine tasters in that they are often able to pinpoint the country of origin, as well as naming the plantation where the coffee was grown.

Cupping—the professional sampling of coffee to insure quality— is a respected art that requires training and experience.

COFFEES BY COUNTRY

Do you remember when just about all coffee was sold in cans, and all came from the same region of the world? Well, those days are gone, and now you can buy your coffee in cans or bags, whole or ground, from the exotic plantations of far-off Africa or from a neighboring Central American grower. Not sure which coffee is the best match for your tastes? The remainder of this chapter will take you on an around-the-world tour designed to help you find the most satisfying beans for your next cup of Joe.

Central and South American Coffees

When most Americans think of coffee, they think of Colombia. But coffee is grown in many regions of the Americas, providing a wide range of beans with a wide range of characteristics. Whether you like your coffee mild or intense, spicy or winey, you're sure to find a pleasing brew among the following selections.

Colombia

Colombia grows coffee on the mountain ranges that run north and south in the foothills of the Andes. Coffee trees thrive on the well-drained, rich volcanic soil, and are protected from the heat of the relentless sun by the shade of banana and rubber trees. The large coffee plantations are run by cooperatives, but small individual family farms also play an important part. Because the beans ripen at different times throughout the mountain ranges, harvesting takes place throughout the year. The coffees of this region—named after the towns and cities through which they're marketed—include Medillin, Armenia, Manizales, Bogota, and Bucaramanga.

Colombia is the second highest producer of coffee in the world, right after Brazil. Nevertheless, because of its high-quality beans, the Colombian coffee

Grown at high altitudes and tended with painstaking care, Colombian coffee is among the best in the world—rich, full-bodied, and perfectly balanced.

The Best Coffee in the World

According to the New York Board of Trade, parent company of the Coffee, Sugar & Cocoa Exchange, Colombian coffee is the best in the world. When judging coffee, the Exchange issues a Notice of Certification based on a testing of the bean grade as well as a tasting of the coffee. Certain coffees—the "Basis" coffees in the table at right—are employed as a benchmark, and a point system is used to grade coffees typical of the countries in which they are grown. When compared with the base coffees, some coffees are judged premium and some are judged inferior. The following table includes the results of one judging, showing how the Exchange rated a selection of coffees from around the world. See if you agree.

**SELECTED COFFEE RATINGS
BY THE NEW YORK BOARD OF TRADE**

Country of Origin	Rating
Mexico, Salvador, Guatemala, Costa Rica, Nicaragua, Kenya, New Guinea, Tanzania, Uganda, Panama	Basis
Colombia	Plus 200 points
Honduras, Venezuela	Minus 100 points
Burundi, India, Rwanda	Minus 300 points
Dominican Republic, Ecuador, Peru	Minus 400 points

industry is considered the giant of the mild coffee-producing countries, and its product is appreciated worldwide. (To learn how Colombian coffee is rated, see the inset above.) High-grade Colombian arabica—the best of which is called *supremo*—delivers a rich cup, full-bodied, and brimming with smooth, intense coffee flavor that has the perfect balance of acidity and mellowness. The finest of the beans have a slightly winey edge.

Brazil

With more than 4 billion coffee trees covering the hills of Brazil, this country produces more coffee than any other nation on the planet—30 to 35 percent of the world's yield. You may remember that many of Brazil's coffee plantations were established in the early 1700s. Their origins date back to coffee plant seedlings that came from the Arbre Mère—the Mother Tree—given to the French King Louis XIV by the Dutch. For a long time, the coffees of Brazil were used primarily in blends and didn't command much respect. However, that changed in the early 1990s when the government relinquished control of the industry. Quality coffees are now being produced with an eye to the international market.

Because Brazil's coffee is exported all over the world, any reduction in its harvest has worldwide effects. Most often, these reductions are caused by the rare but devastating frosts experienced in the areas where coffee plantations are found. You'll know when these climatic emergencies occur because you'll find yourself paying more at the supermarket.

Although coffee is produced throughout Brazil, the highest-grade beans—known as Brazilian Santos or Bourbon Santos—come from the Sao Paulo region. When given a medium roast, these popular beans produce a smooth, mild cup of coffee with medium body and moderate acidity.

Bourbon Santos coffee, the highest grade of Brazilian beans, is produced by the Bourbon strain of the coffee tree for only three or four years. After that, the beans grow larger, flatter, and lower in quality, at which point they are referred to as Flat Bean Santos.

Costa Rica

The first coffee trees were planted in Costa Rica in the late 1770s. Most plantations are situated in the countryside surrounding the capital of San José, where the nutrient-rich volcanic soil is well-drained. In this area, the yield of beans per acre is the highest in the world. Coffee beans grown above 3,900 feet are graded as SHB, or Strictly Hard Bean. From 3,300 feet to 3,900 feet, the beans are graded GHB, or Good Hard Bean. These distinctions are important because the cool air found at higher elevations causes the coffee cherries to ripen more slowly, giving the final brew a rich, hearty flavor that is the hallmark of fine Costa Rican coffee.

Costa Rica produces slow-ripening classic arabica beans, with a robust richness, mellow taste, and exceptionally full body. If you have a choice, opt for Tres Rios, which is mild and sweet; Tarrazu, which is mellow yet full-bodied; and Alajuela, which is crisply acidic but well-balanced.

Guatemala

In Guatemala, coffee was first grown as an ornamental plant by Jesuit priests in the late 1700s, and was not recognized as a money-maker for nearly a century. In the late 1800s, a few indigo planters switched to coffee when the market for indigo collapsed. Most of Guatemala's coffee today is grown by the Maya who live in Atitlan, where the soil is rich and well-drained. The Strictly Hard Bean, or SHB, coffee is grown above 4,500 feet; while the Hard Bean, or HB, coffee is produced between 4,000 and 4,500 feet. As in Costa Rica, the coolness of the air slows the ripening of the coffee cherries, promoting full-bodied flavor in the cup.

> Antigua and Coban coffees are generally recognized as the finest that Guatemala has to offer. Some experts, though, feel that the less-celebrated Huehuetenango beans are also excellent.

The best Guatemalan coffees are considered to be Antigua and Coban. These arabica beans produce a medium-bodied brew with high acidity and a slightly spicy, smoky flavor that sets Guatemalan coffee apart from all others.

Mexico

Mexico is the fourth largest producer of coffee in the world. The Spanish brought coffee seedlings to Mexico in the late 1700s and established small plantations in the central highlands, where they continue to flourish today. Commercial coffee manufacturers often use Mexican beans for blending purposes because their delicacy does not add distinctive flavor, but helps amplify the flavor of any beans with which they are mated. Farming practices on the large cooperatives are improving the quality of the beans, and the family farms are following suit. A recently formed trade association is becoming successful in promoting Mexican coffees in the marketplace.

The best Mexican coffee beans come from Oaxaca and Veracruz. Be on the lookout for Oaxaca State, Oaxaca Pluma, and Altura Coatepec from Veracruz. These beans produce a brew that is light-bodied, with a dry, acidic snap.

Nicaragua

For a period of time in the 1980s, Nicaraguan coffee was not imported into the United States because of political differences between the two governments. Now Nicaraguan coffee is available again. However, the country's agricultural fortunes have suffered from natural disasters over the years, and the harvest has been scant. It will take time for the seedlings to grow to maturity. Nicaragua is the poorest country in Central America, and coffee is its major export. The hope is that the industry will continue to grow and improve.

Serious coffee drinkers believe that Nicaraguan coffees are undervalued in the world market. The mountains of the north and central regions of the country produce the best-quality arabicas, which are grouped together as Central Estrictamente Altura. If you have the opportunity, choose a high-grown coffee like Jinotega or Matagalpa. These coffees are mild and smooth with a medium to light body and a lovely aroma.

African Coffees

Coffee drinkers used to mild South American blends will be struck by the difference between their everyday brew and those produced in Africa. These coffees are characterized by wine-like and/or fruity overtones with bright acidity. In addition, they usually have an intense flavor that makes them sought after by true coffee aficionados.

Mexican coffee has been compared to a light white wine. At its best, it is dry and delicate in body, with an acidic snap.

Ethiopia

Of course, you know that Ethiopia is the birthplace of coffee, and wild coffee is still found thriving on the mountainsides. Family farms are mixed in with modern coffee plantations, and most of the beans are grown at elevations of 5,000 feet. In one way or another, at least a quarter of the population is involved in coffee production. Simply everyone drinks coffee every day. In fact, Ethiopians consume more coffee than the people of any other African nation.

Connoisseurs seek out Ethiopian coffees because of the deep, true coffee flavor of their arabica beans. Expect a slightly bitter, full-bodied cupful with a winey taste, a hint of spice, and a strong aroma. Look for Ethiopian Harrar Longberry, which has a distinctive aromatic character, and Ethiopian Yirgacheffe, which ranks among the best in the world.

Kenya

Coffee arrived in Kenya from the Island of Reunion in the late 1800s, but it was not until the 1900s that the crop was cultivated in earnest, first by the Germans, and then by the British. The benign climate allows two harvests per year. Most of the farms are situated at elevations of between 5,000 and 7,000 feet, with the main growing area extending south from the slopes of Mount Kenya almost to the capital of Nairobi. The majority of the Kenyan coffee sold in specialty stores comes from that area, rather than the smaller coffee-growing region on the slopes of Mount Elgon.

There are no Kenyan estate coffees because the beans are sold by grade at weekly auctions in Nairobi. The highest-quality beans command the highest prices at these auctions.

Kenyan coffees are consistently good. When given a medium roast, they have intense coffee flavor, with a smoky hint of wine and just a bit of a bite. A light roast leaves behind too much acidity, and a dark roast masks the flavor of

Coffee Tasting Terms

At one time or another, you've probably described a coffee as being "bitter" or as having great "body." But when professional tasters analyze different coffees, they draw on an extensive lexicon of terms, each of which has a very precise meaning. Intrigued? The following sampling of terms will let you in on just a few of the characteristics that tasters look for when they enter a cupping room.

acidity. A sensation created when the acids in the coffee combine with the sugars, resulting in the overall sweetness of the beverage. Coffees that lack acidity taste dull and flat.

aged. A term used to describe green coffee beans that have been stored for a specific period of time to produce a mellow flavor and good body.

aroma. The smell of brewed coffee, which can be described as lacking aroma or as having faint, delicate, moderate, strong, or pungent aroma.

bitter. An unpleasantly harsh flavor detected on the back of the tongue. This may be caused by a variety of factors, including overroasting.

body. The sensation of coffee in the mouth, ranging from thin to light, medium, full, heavy, and syrupy.

caramelly. An aromatic sensation reminiscent of caramelized sugar, produced by the sugar compounds in the coffee.

coarse. A flavor that is raspy and harsh.

earthy. A flavor of wet earth that results from improper storage of coffee beans.

fiery. A charcoal flavor generally caused by over-roasting.

flat. A flavor that is lifeless and lacking in acidity.

flavor. The taste and smell of coffee, resulting from the combined impression of aroma, acidity, and body.

fruity. A strong, overly ripe flavor.

grassy. A flavor that is greenish, indicating that the coffee beans were picked before reaching optimum ripeness.

harsh. An unpleasantly rough, sharp, or irritating flavor.

light. A term used to signify either a delicate flavor or a lack of aroma, acidity, or body.

malty. A flavor or aroma reminiscent of toasted grains.

mellow. A flavor that is well-balanced, full, and smooth, but lacking in acidity.

muddy. A flavor that is dull and indistinct, possibly due to the grounds being agitated.

nutty. An aroma reminiscent of roasted nuts.

rich. A term used to describe coffee that has depth and complexity of flavor and body.

smooth. A term used to describe coffee that is full-bodied but low in acid.

soft. A flavor that is well-rounded and lacking in harshness or acidity.

spicy. A flavor or aroma suggestive of spices.

stale. A flavor that is sweet but unpleasant, implying that the coffee is past its prime.

sweet. A flavor that is pleasant, clean, smooth, and free from bitterness or harshness.

thin. A term used to describe coffee that is flat, lifeless, and lacking in body.

winey. A rich, rounded, smooth flavor reminiscent of mature red wine.

woody. A woodlike flavor that may result from the coffee being stored too long as green beans.

the coffee. Those in the know consider Cooper & Company's Kenya AA the best of the country's offerings.

Tanzania

Tanzania has the right climate, much land, and enough labor to establish high-quality coffee farms. Most Tanzanian arabica plants are grown on the slopes of Mount Kilimanjaro and Mount Meru, near the border. Smaller amounts are grown father south, between Lake Tanganyika and Lake Nyasa. The principal challenge faced by coffee growers in this country is the need to develop disease-resistant coffee trees that won't fall victim to pests. Due to these continuing difficulties, harvests are low. However, the potential is there, and this African country may yet become a major player in the industry.

Although Tanzanian coffees are similar to Kenyan coffees, they generally have less acidity. The ones to seek out are Kilimanjaro and Kibo, both of which are named for the mountains on which they are grown. (Kibo is an extinct volcano on Kilimanjaro.) These coffees are well-balanced and full of flavor with a superb aroma; they are great favorites of the Japanese. If you stumble upon Tanzanian Peaberry, buy it immediately. It is smooth and full-bodied with a hint of spiciness.

Arabian Coffee

When we talk about Arabian coffee, we're really talking about the coffee of Yemen. Aside from the wild coffee plants of Ethiopia, discussed earlier in the chapter, Arabian Mocha is the most ancient coffee—and is considered one of the best. Mocha is still grown in North Yemen as it has been for hundreds of years, and the beans are processed as they have been for centuries. The old ways are also observed in the making of the coffee. The people of Yemen brew *kahwe* from barely roasted beans spiced with cardamom, ginger, cloves, or cinnamon. Fully roasted beans are reserved for celebrations, as they have been since ancient times.

Like African coffees, the coffee of Yemen has true coffee flavor with winey overtones and good acidity. The best of the beans are the Mocha Yemen Mattari, which brew into a wonderful full-flavored, full-bodied cup with a tantalizing hint of chocolate. Yemenite coffees are diverse in taste because of the varied climatic conditions found within this small country. Some are smooth and almost fruity; some are bitter and chocolatey; some are earthy and heavy. But all the coffees of Yemen are marvelously distinct in flavor.

Arabian Mocha, from North Yemen, is still grown as it has been for centuries—on terraces shaded from the desert sun by rows of poplar trees. Irrigation is provided by rock-lined channels that direct the water to the roots of the plants.

Island Coffees

Coffees from the Islands are known for their well-balanced acidity; full body; and smooth, rich flavor. However, they also offer great variety, for while one has delightfully fruity notes, another provides a pleasantly smoky taste, giving the coffee lover a range of brews to sample, compare, and enjoy.

Hawaii

Coffee has been grown in Hawaii since the early 1800s. There are more than 600 coffee plantations in Kona—the west-central coast of Hawaii Island—covering around 2,000 acres, and producing 2 million or so pounds of beans annually. The Big Island also has coffee farms at Kau and Hamakau. Coffee is also grown on Hawaii's smaller islands. Oahu grows beans on more than 100 acres, Molokai grows coffee on 450 acres, Maui has scattered coffee farms, and Kauai boasts the largest coffee plantation in the United States.

The Kona coast produces a unique, very desirable coffee of incomparable lightness and sweetness. The taste is rich, yet mild; full-bodied, yet light; with a natural almost floral acidity and a wonderful aroma. Be aware that coffees marked "Kona Blend" may contain only 5 percent actual Kona, and look for undiluted Kona to savor this marvelous coffee in all its glory.

Jamaica

Other West Indian islands grow coffee, but Jamaican coffee is far and away the best, as well as the best known. It's interesting that Jamaica actually produces two types of coffee. Its lowland coffee is so ordinary that it appears in the United States only as fillers for cheap blends. And then there's the highland coffee—the famous Jamaican Blue Mountain, which ranks among the world's best. The legendary Blue Mountains run from roughly from the center of

Jamaica and meander toward the southeastern tip of the island. This is where about 15,000 acres of coffee trees thrive at 7,000 feet, making Jamaican Blue Mountain the highest-grown coffee in the world.

The perfectly balanced Jamaican Blue Mountain is a full-bodied, richly flavorful, sweet and almost fruity coffee, with an incomparable aroma that teases the taste buds. To sniff while it's brewing is to enjoy the promise of pleasures to come. Blue Mountain coffee is hard to find because most of the production goes to the Japanese, and the 10 percent that's left is divided among the United States, United Kingdom, and Germany. If you find it, treasure it. Look for Wallensford Estate coffee, High Mountain Supreme, and Prime Washed Jamaican.

Jamaican Blue Mountain is perhaps the world's most celebrated coffee— smooth, full-bodied, and rich.

Java

After gaining control of the region in the 1600s and 1700s, Dutch settlers brought arabica beans to Java and established massive plantations. Although the original trees fell victim to disease in the 1870s and robusta trees were substituted, high-quality arabica trees are once again flourishing on Java.

Javanese beans are aged for several years in special warehouses, where they turn from pale green to brown. In the old days, the beans traveled by clipper ship to their destinations and matured to a mellow richness during the trip. As time went on, clients complained of a raw taste when the beans arrived too quickly. Aging the beans before shipment solved the problem, and the Indonesians have been doing it ever since, producing a rich and mellow taste in the cup, with less acidity than that found in fresh-roasted beans, and a flavor that is almost nutty and slightly smoky. You might see these coffees marked "passage beans," referring to the aging process that mimics the "passage" they once took by ship, or they might be called Old Java, Aged Java, or Old Brown Java. If you haven't yet tried Javanese coffee, keep an eye out for it.

New Guinea

The history of coffee in New Guinea is short and sweet. Production began in the 1950s, and small coffee farms are scattered from 4,000 to 6,000 feet. The industry continues to expand, however, and quality continues to improve, with most of the coffee coming from Papua New Guinea, which occupies the eastern half of the New Guinea island.

The coffees of New Guinea resemble Kenyan coffees, which is not surprising as the trees were established with Kenyan root stock. Papouasie is a fine, full-bodied arabica—smooth and mellow, with just a hint of acidity and a nice aroma.

Sumatra

Although the coffees of Hawaii and Jamaica may be the most famous, many experts consider Sumatra's Mandheling and Ankola the world's finest—full-bodied with a rich, smooth, vibrant flavor.

Once their plantations on Java were established, the Dutch brought seedlings to Sumatra and the coffee farms flourished. The Sumatran climate is well-suited to coffee production, with the best crops growing at altitudes of 2,500 to 5,000 feet. The west coast of Sumatra produces arabica beans, while the eastern region of the island is devoted to robusta beans.

Sumatra's best medium-roasted arabica beans deliver intense, full-bodied coffee flavor with low acidity, a hint of sweetness, and an earthy taste. The aroma is wonderful, too. If you haven't tried Sumatran coffee, look for Mandheling and Ankola beans, which are dry milled for concentrated flavor. You're in for a taste treat.

India

You may remember that Chapter 1 recounted the story of Baba Budan, the Indian trader who is credited with smuggling fertile coffee seeds out of Arabia and planting them in southern India—or so the legend goes. That was in the

1600s, but the coffee plantations of India weren't cultivated in earnest until the 1800s. The tropical weather and rich soil proved ideal for coffee, as well as spices. Both are primary exports of India.

The Monsooned Malabar coffee of India is a connoisseur's delight. Tradition dictates that the dried beans be exposed to monsoon winds to mimic the flavor that developed when the beans were transported by clipper ship, a trip that took several months. If you're lucky enough to find this premium coffee, expect a creamy cupful with light acidity, a spicy aroma, and a delicious mellowed richness of flavor.

Kopi Luwak Coffee

Earlier in the book, I promised that this chapter would take you from the sublime to the ridiculous. If coffees from Colombia and Kona are sublime, Kopi Luwak coffee must be ridiculous.

By the early 1700s, the Dutch controlled Java's burgeoning coffee plantations. There, a tree-dwelling animal called the Paradoxus, or palm civet, became quite a pest to coffee growers when it climbed into the coffee trees and ate only the ripest, reddest coffee cherries. However, the civet digested the beans only partially, so locals separated the coffee cherries from the scat (droppings) of the civet and tried them out. Ridiculous? Maybe, but coffee brewed from beans partially digested and dropped by the civet is said to be unique, with a syrupy caramel taste, a heavy body, and incomparable richness. Kopi Luwak now comes from Java, Sumatra, and Sulawesi, which are all part of the Indonesian Archipelago's island chain.

Kopi Luwak is expensive—about $175 per pound—and hard to find. But if you want a taste of something truly rare and you're not put off by the beans' origin, try searching the Internet, where you'll find Kopi Luwak beans offered for sale.

Kopi Luwak is certainly the rarest coffee in the world, with only about 500 pounds being produced each year. The reason? Kopi Luwak beans are partially predigested by the palm civet, a tree-dwelling animal that eats the cherries off the coffee trees and then excretes them, leaving them to be gathered and processed.

Hopefully, by now you've homed in on the beans that will most perfectly match your tastes. In the next chapter, you'll learn how to take those carefully selected beans and turn them into the best possible brew—one that will showcase the coffee you have chosen and satisfy all of your expectations.

CHAPTER 6

Making the Best **Brew**

Make my coffee strong!

—CHARLES MACKAY (1814–1889)

While the writer quoted above might have preferred his coffee strong, you may fancy a milder brew. But regardless of the desired strength, you surely want your coffee to be the best it can be—fresh, hot, and flavorful, with no hint of bitterness. If this is what you've always aimed for, but it's *not* what you've been getting, this chapter should help. It starts off with guidelines for buying, storing, and grinding coffee; continues with tips for selecting a coffeemaker; and concludes with valuable advice on brewing. The result should be the most delicious cup of Joe you've ever enjoyed in your own home.

SELECTING THE COFFEE

For a very long time, most people were content with one of the many vacuum-packed brand-name coffees found on supermarket shelves—and for a long time, that's all that was available in most areas. But now, far more options exist for the coffee aficionado. Coffeehouses, specialty stores, and mail-order companies now offer a wide variety of high-quality products, both ground and whole bean. And even supermarkets carry a range of choices, including several different roasts, a selection of flavored products, and—for the person with no time to spare—single-serving packets and instant coffees. Decisions, decisions!

Specialty Coffees

The concept of gourmet coffee has its roots in Europe, where select beans have been imported and roasted by specialty shops since the 1800s. But not until the last few decades of the twentieth century did North Americans begin demanding high-quality beans roasted with the utmost care.

In Chapter 5, you learned about some of the deliciously different coffees now available from around the world. I hope that you've sampled some of them by now. If not, I encourage you to do so posthaste. Most coffeehouses and specialty stores and many supermarkets now offer a wide selection of specialty coffees—high-quality beans that have been roasted with care. You'll find the beans displayed in closed bins with their origins—Kenya, Sumatra, Hawaii, and the like—clearly labeled. Specialty shops do the grinding for you, but most supermarkets have grinders available for your use.

Many selections of specialty coffees include flavored beans, which have been steadily gaining favor since they were introduced in the mid-1970s. To create this product, roasters spray green coffee beans with a micromist of a flavored solution before the roasting begins. The tiny droplets are so fine that they're almost invisible, and the measuring is precise. Too little and the flavor will be weak; too much, and the flavor will be so pronounced that it will mask the taste of the coffee.

Today you can choose from an amazing number of flavored coffees, both caffeinated and decaffeinated. Among the most popular are Irish Cream, with a hint of Irish Cream whiskey; French Vanilla, with a suggestion of vanilla; and several chocolate-infused brews, such as Chocolate Raspberry. Although flavored coffees may be enjoyed at any time, all of them are so rich-tasting that I think of them as dessert-in-a-cup.

While specialty coffee shops provide a wonderful sensory experience, with their piles of glossy beans and their intoxicating aromas, there is a drawback. By displaying the beans in bins—which normally lack tight seals—shopkeepers unavoidably expose them to the air. Oxygen gradually diminishes the flavor of coffee and, over time, it can develop a stale taste. I always hope the shop or market sells a lot of coffee and replenishes its bins often so that the beans are freshly roasted, but unfortunately, there's no way to be certain that the coffee isn't stale when you buy it. The best strategy is to find a busy shop with a solid reputation. Then buy only small amounts of beans until you've confirmed that the store's selection and quality meet your needs and standards.

To insure that your specialty beans are as fresh and flavorful as they should be, buy your coffee from a busy shop that has a solid reputation, and purchase only a small amount at a time.

Brand-Name Coffees

You may be surprised to learn that the first ground, roasted coffee, Ariosa, was made commercially available in 1865. Soon, others jumped on the bandwagon, and before World War I, a slew of companies—Hills Brothers, Maxwell House, and Eight O'Clock among them—were well established. Now, of course, every supermarket offers a wide variety of brands, in both cans and brick-packs.

While the specialty coffees discussed earlier are often single-source high-quality beans, roasted to perfection in small batches, many brand-name commercial coffees are a blend of medium-grade arabica beans and less expensive robusta beans, and are roasted in giant machines. While this may sound discouraging, keep in mind that brand-name coffees have some advantages, as

Premium Coffees—
The Best of the Specialty Beans

The high-quality beans available from specialty shops and mail-order companies almost always deliver a good cup of coffee. But there's no doubt that some specialty coffees are better than others. The best coffees—the premium coffees—are usually single-source arabica beans that have been produced in small batches in what's known as a fluid air bed roaster. This method tumbles the beans in a roasting chamber that has continuously circulating super-heated air. Unlike the direct heat method, the sides of the roasting chamber are never hot enough to burn the beans. Each bean is equally roasted, never scorched and never underdone. Another advantage of this method is that circulating air blows the chaff (silverskin) away from the beans through the chaff cyclone, a specially designed separate compartment, where it falls into what's called a chaff can. Air roasting thus produces a clean roast every time.

The optimum type of roast is dictated by the origin of the beans, and it's not done by the clock. The roasting process is carefully watched by a roastmaster who pulls out samples of the beans during the roast. The roastmaster both eyes and smells the beans to determine when the proper color and aroma have been achieved. The result is a superior bean and, ultimately, full, rich flavor in your cup.

well. Commercial coffees are carefully controlled to insure that every can of coffee you buy has a uniform taste. So if you have a favorite brand, by all means, enjoy it. When compared with specialty coffees, vacuum-packed cans of brand-name coffees deliver excellent value for a modest price.

Instant Coffee

Although pulverized coffee was available as early as the eighteenth century, the first modern instant coffee was created in the 1930s by Nestlé, and their product, Nescafé, was offered for sale in 1938. Originally, instant coffee was made through spray-drying—a process Nestlé had developed for the manufacture of powdered milk. But following World War II, the freeze-drying process was developed, producing a superior product that caused the popularity of instant coffee to skyrocket.

Some instant coffees—including the so-called "International" products—are now available in flavors. While many people love these sweet, easy-to-make specialty beverages, be aware that the ingredients include very little coffee, and a whole slew of artificial ingredients and hydrogenated oils. So if you're interested in a purer product with truer coffee taste, unflavored instants are a far better option.

Instant coffee remains a choice for coffee lovers who lack the time to brew a pot. When you want a cup of coffee, all you need do is stir a spoonful of the dry coffee crystals into freshly-boiled water. Each cup tastes just like the one before it because the blend of beans is carefully controlled. While the resulting beverage lacks the full flavor and character of a freshly brewed cup, the convenience of instant coffee cannot be denied.

Instant coffee can be a real lifesaver when you want to make a cup of Joe without the fuss of brewing a pot, or when you want to add intense coffee flavor to baked goods, puddings, or sauces.

Single-Cup Servings

For many years, instant coffee has not been the only option for coffee drinkers who want a fast cup of Joe. Now, coffee "tea bags" that "brew" in the cup are available for those who drink only an occasional cup of coffee, as well as for travelers who lack the luxury of a coffeepot. The bags—referred to by various names, including "singles"—contain ground coffee plus, in many cases, concentrated coffee. Many people find the taste of the final brew a bit fresher than that of instant. Single-cup bags can be used in a cup of boiling water or with the help of a microwave oven.

Flavorings for Coffee

In addition to the many coffees now available for sale—and often alongside them—you'll find selected flavorings in either liquid form or as small "buttons" about the size of an aspirin. A tablespoon of liquid syrup or one small "button" is all it takes to infuse a single cup of coffee with a burst of flavor. These flavorings—which include vanilla, raspberry-chocolate, hazelnut, and more—allow you to customize unflavored coffee to suit your own tastes or those of your guests.

While specially made coffee flavorings are fun, don't overlook the coffee flavorings you probably already have on the shelves of your pantry. Ground cinnamon or nutmeg, lightly sprinkled over grounds before brewing, can add a subtle, all-natural flavor to your coffee. Another option is to add unsweetened cocoa to the grounds. When used sparingly—only about a half teaspoon to a pot—cocoa can eliminate the bitterness in coffee, producing a rich, mellow brew.

A Word on Blending

Many coffee lovers enjoy making their own custom blends, using either whole bean or ground coffee. Try mixing light roasts and dark roasts, or add just a few scoops of flavored coffee to your favorite unflavored brand.

In Chapter 2, you learned how some coffee companies blend beans from different origins to create certain classic blends or to achieve more uniform results even when supply conditions change. But, of course, many people create their own special coffee blends at home. Try combining equal parts of Mocha and Java coffees to make your own Mocha Java blend. Add a few scoops of a deep-roast coffee to a lighter roast to deepen the flavor. Or mix a few spoonfuls of expensive premium coffee with canned coffee to produce a richer, more interesting cup. Keep notes on your experiments, and you may find that you can create a "house" blend that not only suits your tastes to a T, but is also kind to your pocketbook.

STORING THE COFFEE

As mentioned earlier in the chapter, coffee is a highly perishable commodity. As soon as the beans are roasted, they begin releasing carbon dioxide and other gases. This permits the absorption of oxygen and moisture, which fades the flavor and eventually causes the coffee oils to turn rancid. Vacuum-packed cans or vacuum-packed bags can preserve the freshness almost indefinitely, but coffee begins to deteriorate as soon as the packaging is opened. And, of course, coffee purchased in coffeehouses and specialty stores often comes in paper sacks that do little to safeguard the flavor of the beans.

Because fresh beans are key to good coffee, seriously consider the option of buying your coffee in whole bean rather than ground form. The whole beans have less surface area to permit the escape of gases and the absorption of flavor-robbing air. Simply put, whole beans keep better and lose less aroma than ground. Realize, though, that even whole beans don't keep forever; once they've been roasted, their oils break through cell walls, exposing them to the ravages of oxygen. But if you buy your beans whole and grind them just before you brew, your coffee will be far fresher than that made from preground beans. (You'll learn more about grinding later in the chapter.)

Whether you buy your beans whole or ground, try to purchase small amounts—ideally, only as much you can use in a week. Then store the coffee in an airtight moisture-proof container in your freezer. The container will protect the coffee from the air, and the freezing will slow down the biological processes that cause coffee to deteriorate. Stored this way, freshly roasted whole beans will keep well for up to four weeks, and ground coffee will retain its flavor for up to two weeks. Don't store your coffee in the refrigerator, though. Any moisture that develops from condensation will adversely affect the beans.

Whether ground or whole, there is no need to defrost the beans before

Every coffee expert offers advice on preserving the freshness of coffee through proper storage. But perhaps the best advice is this: Buy only as much coffee as you can drink in a week.

brewing. Simply place the frozen grounds in the coffeemaker, or transfer the frozen whole beans directly to your home grinder.

GRINDING THE BEANS

The grinding of coffee beans—when they're ground and how finely they're ground—has a huge effect on the final brew. As you just learned, for maximum flavor and freshness, coffee should ideally be ground right before it's prepared. Just as important, the particle size must match the way in which the coffee will be made. The finer the beans are ground, the more quickly the flavor will be extracted from the beans during brewing. That is why espresso is ground so finely, while the appropriate grind for a drip pot is far coarser. Keep this in mind whether you have your beans ground in a specialty store or you grind them yourself at home.

If you do decide to maximize flavor by grinding your coffee beans right in your own kitchen, you can choose between two types of grinders—the electric blade grinder and the burr grinder. Each has its advantages and disadvantages.

The Electric Blade Grinder

Most people who grind at home use an electric blade grinder, also referred to as a propeller grinder. As the name implies, this device consists of a rotating blade set inside a container. (Think of a small blender.) The coffee beans are simply put in the container, where the whirring blades chop them up.

While these grinders are fast, convenient, and inexpensive—you can pick up a blade grinder for $20 to $30—they do have drawbacks, the most important being the lack of consistency. The coffee beans that are "ground" first continue to be processed as the machine runs, getting smaller and smaller as the remaining beans wait to be ground. This results in particles that are uneven in size, which leads to a less-than-perfect brew. In addition, few or no blade grinders can process beans finely enough for espresso.

The Burr Grinder

The burr grinder—also called the burr mill or coffee mill—has two metal discs, or burrs, that face each other, and can be adjusted to create grinds of different sizes. Coffee beans are fed through the discs, a few at a time. The ground beans then fall into a compartment below, out of the way of the discs.

The advantage of the burr grinder is clear. The results are the same every time, giving you a consistently good brew. In addition, the different settings available on most mills allow you to grind beans precisely for any coffeemaker, including an espresso machine. However, there are also disadvantages. Because the beans must pass through the discs at a fixed rate, burr grinders work more slowly than blade grinders. They are also noisier than blade grinders, and can be messy to operate. And burr grinders can be expensive, running from $50 to $100. But if you want your coffee beans ground to perfection, this is your best option.

Although burr grinders are somewhat slow, and are far more costly than their electric blade counterparts, they enable you to precisely match your coffee grind to the needs of your coffeemaker.

The Proper Grind

To a degree, you will have to rely on trial and error to find the proper grind for your coffeemaker. While some people might prefer a slightly coarser grind, you might prefer a slightly finer grind—even though you're both using the same pot. However, as explained earlier, the type of coffeemaker you use is the most important deciding factor in choosing a grind. The less time the grounds will be in contact with the water, the finer the grounds must be to allow all of the beans' flavor to be extracted. The following table will guide you in determining the best grind for your own coffeemaker. Most burr grinders allow you

CHOOSING THE BEST COFFEE GRIND	
Type of Coffeemaker	**Recommended Grind**
Percolators and commercial urns.	Coarse grind. If you're using a blade grinder, process for five to seven seconds.
Plunger pots and electric drip pots.	Medium grind. If you're using a blade grinder, process for about ten seconds.
Manual drip pots and espresso machines.	Fine grind. If you're using a blade grinder, process for fifteen to twenty seconds.
Ibriks, vacuum pots, and some older espresso machines.	Extra-fine grind. If you're using a blade grinder, process for twenty-five to thirty seconds.

to set the machine for the desired grind. If you're using a blade grinder, though, this table will help you gauge the amount of processing time needed to reach the preferred consistency.

SELECTING A COFFEEMAKER

High-quality, fresh coffee beans—ground exactly right—are central to the making of a good brew. But without a coffeemaker, you still don't have a cup of Joe.

The selection of a coffeemaker is a personal choice. Only you know how you like your coffee, how much you want to spend on coffee-making equipment, and how much fuss you want to go to every time you brew a pot. The following information is designed to guide you to a maker that you will find convenient and affordable, and that will produce a brew that you will enjoy day in and day out.

The Percolator

A percolator is designed to hold the coffee grounds in a metal basket that sits

How much money are you willing to spend on brewing equipment? How much time can you devote to making your coffee? Do you drink your coffee as soon as it's brewed, or do you sip it throughout the morning? Be sure to consider all these points before choosing your next coffeemaker.

atop a hollow stem. Then, whether powered by electricity or the heat of a stovetop, boiling water is forced up through the stem and sprayed over the grounds. The water then drips slowly through the coffee grounds into the pot below, where it is again heated and forced upwards, over the grounds.

A great deal of controversy has sprung up around the humble percolator. While some coffee lovers extol the virtues of a percolated brew, others condemn it for being acrid. The problem is that the percolator continually pumps the *same* liquid through the grounds, and boils it over and over again to create sufficient pressure to force it back up the stem. Experts say that this process burns off the delicate aromatics of the beans, producing a bitter, poorly balanced beverage. If you nonetheless love the taste of perked coffee, you'll be happy to know that an automatic percolator costs only around $30.

A housewife of Dresden, Germany, Melitta Bentz invented the first coffee filter in 1908, using her son's blotter paper.

The Manual Drip Pot

You may be interested to know that the world's first drip coffeemaker was invented in 1908. That same year, Melitta Bentz came up with a filter to keep the gritty grounds out of the finished brew. And the manual drip pot is still being enthusiastically used today.

In this simple coffeemaker, ground coffee is placed in a filter suspended above a carafe. Freshly boiled water is allowed to cool slightly, and then poured slowly over the ground coffee, which it drips through on its way to the carafe below.

Many people love this type of coffeemaker, as the method is easy and the pot itself is highly portable. The disadvantages, however, are clear. The water must be boiled separately and added to the pot, and the coffee-

Manual Drip Pot

making process takes longer than it does in many electric pots. Additionally, this pot is not designed to keep the coffee hot once it's been brewed. However, because of its simplicity, this coffeemaker is highly affordable—about $25.

The Electric Drip Pot

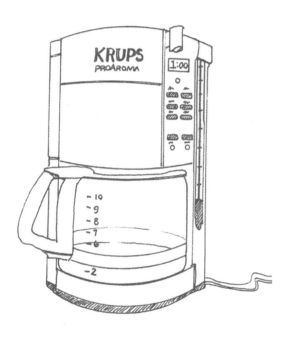

Electric Drip Pot

This pot works by the same principle as the manual drip. Grounds are placed in a filter, and water in a reservoir. From this point on, though, the coffeemaker takes over, heating the water to the correct temperature and funneling it through the coffee. The resulting mixture drips into a glass coffee pot, which sits on a warming plate.

Although clearly not as portable as a manual drip pot, the electric drip is probably the most popular coffeemaker in the United States simply because it is so easy to use and because its warming plate prevents the coffee from growing cold. The catch is that it does this by continually heating the coffee, a process that can leave your coffee sour and bitter. In addition, some aficionados claim that when paper rather than metal filters are used, flavorful oils end up in the filter rather than the brewed coffee, where they belong. (The same can be said for the manual drip pot, by the way.)

Electric drip coffeemakers abound. Depending on their features, they range in price from $30 to around $80—the price of a coffeemaker that has a charcoal water filter and a heating element that uses low heat to keep coffee hot for up to two hours.

Turkish Delights

In Chapter 3, you read about the coffeehouses of Constantinople, where thick, sweet coffee was enjoyed as early as the 1400s. Turkish coffee is made now just as it's been prepared for centuries—in a special coffeemaker called an ibrik.

Actually, to be fair, the ibrik—or ibriq, as it is sometimes spelled—was originally an Arabian invention, and only later came to be known as a Turkish coffeepot. Also in the name of fairness, it's important to note that in Greece, the same brew made in the ibrik is known as Greek coffee. But for the purpose of clarity, the term Turkish coffee will be used here.

A description of an ibrik written in the seventeenth century by a traveling Frenchman named Dufour survives. Here it is, as written:

In the Levant, for cooking coffee they use a type of kettle made of copper, tinned inside and out, of a rather particular design, which has still not been duplicated in France. They call it an ibriq. I've found it quite suitable for this purpose, since the base, which is broad, receives more of the flame, in consequence of which the water boils more quickly. Additionally, the opening is quite narrow, to better retain the volatile essence of the brew.

Now as then, a Turkish ibrik is a small long-handled coffee pot traditionally made of copper or brass. The best way to determine the capacity of your ibrik is to add water to the pot just to the level of the spout. Then pour the water into small cups to determine how many cups the pot will hold. Don't overfill the pot or the coffee may boil over. This method of brewing requires that the coffee boil and bubble up three times.

The traditional way to brew coffee in an ibrik is to put the water in the pot along with one heaping teaspoon of sugar for each cupful you wish to make. When the sugar water boils, remove the ibrik from the heat and stir in one heaping teaspoon of very finely ground (almost powdered) coffee for each cup of water.

Return the pot to the heat and bring to a boil once more. Then take the pot off the heat again and allow the mixture to settle.

Return the ibrik to the heat once more, and let the mixture bubble up again. Immediately pour a little of the froth into each cup.

Return the ibrik to the heat for the last time, and bring to a boil. Let the mixture settle before pouring the coffee into the cups.

If you want to make spiced coffee in the Arabian way, when the brew boils up for the second time, add a little vanilla bean, a piece of cinnamon stick, or the crushed seeds from one cardamom pod. Because Turkish coffee is boiled three times, the brew is often bitter. Adding spices, as has been done since ancient times, smoothes and softens the brew and masks the bitterness.

Ibrik

Coffeemaker Plus Grinder

This coffeepot combines a coffee bean grinder with an electric drip coffeemaker. You can select the grind you prefer, from coarse to fine, and turn out fresh-tasting coffee every time, which is then kept at serving temperature on a warming plate. Expect to pay from $240 to $300 for all these features.

Coffeemaker Plus Thermal Carafe

Another combination pot, this one merges an electric drip coffeemaker with a thermal carafe. Thus, instead of dripping the brewed coffee into a glass pot that sits on a warming plate, it funnels it into a carafe that needs no additional heat to keep the coffee at sipping temperature. Many thermal carafe coffeemakers even have a water filter that removes chlorine and other nasty tastes from tap water.

The advantages of this combination are obvious. Without external heat, your coffee always tastes freshly brewed, never scorched or stale. Expect to pay from $80 to $150 for a thermal carafe coffeemaker. After researching this material, I confess I abandoned my old coffeemaker and ordered one of these for myself.

The Plunger Pot

The plunger pot—also called a French press or cafetière—consists of a glass cylinder with a metal rod that extends through the center of both the pot and the domed lid. Protruding from the top of the rod is a handle, while a perforated platform (the plunger) is attached to the bottom and fits snugly inside the glass cylinder.

With the lid and plunger removed, ground coffee is placed in the bottom of the pot. Freshly boiled water is allowed to cool slightly, and then poured slowly into the pot. After four to five minutes, the plunger is pushed slowly down to the bottom of the pot, separating the grounds from the liquid and holding them at the bottom of the pot.

Many people claim that a plunger pot is the best means of insuring a smooth and mellow brew without a hint of bitterness. The coffee is not overbrewed as it can be in a percolator, and no filter interferes with the disbursement of flavorful oils. On the other hand, the coffee must be consumed immediately, as the pot is not designed to keep it at serving temperature. In addition, while some people love the full body created by the sediment that usually ends up in the coffee, others prefer a clearer cup.

Plunger Pot

The price of a glass plunger pot is generally $25 or $30. If you like this method of brewing, go the extra mile and select one that brews into an insulated pot which will keep the coffee hot for up to three hours. For this extra feature, expect to spend between $50 and $60.

The Vacuum Pot

Invented in the mid-1800s, the vacuum pot usually is composed of two glass globes, one of which is set over the other with a connecting tube and filter between them. The globes are suspended over a spirit lamp or other heat source, such as a stovetop. Ground coffee is placed in the upper globe, and cold water is poured into the lower globe to the halfway mark, leaving pressurized air in the other half. The lower globe is then heated, which causes the air to expand, forcing the water up the connecting tube into the upper globe. When the heat is removed, the pressure decreases and the brewed coffee filters into the lower globe.

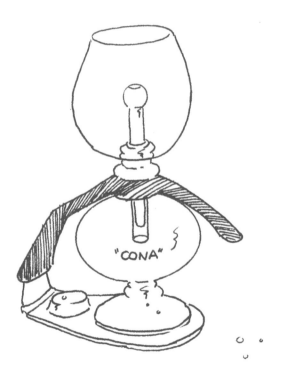

Vacuum Pot

Fragile and requiring both time and painstaking attention, the vacuum pot is not convenient to use. However, many experts judge coffee made in a vacuum pot to be the best possible brew—as sediment-free as drip coffee, yet as full-flavored as that made in a plunger pot, and satisfyingly hot. Depending on the heat source used, on the size of the pot, and on other factors, a vacuum coffeemaker can range from $30 to $250 in price.

The Espresso Machine

The first machine designed to brew espresso—the strong, black coffee favored by the Italians—was created in France in 1882. This early prototype apparently didn't catch on, because in 1905, an Italian manufactured the first commercially successful espresso machine. The first electric espresso maker was manufactured by Dr. Ernest Illy in 1933, but it was Achilles Gaggia who perfected the design. In 1945, he created a espresso maker fitted with a piston that produced a thick layer of *crema*—honey-colored froth—by high-pressure extraction.

Different espresso makers operate in different ways. In general, though, the base of the machine is filled with water, and the filter container with specially ground coffee. Steam and water are then forced under high pressure through the pot to the grounds. When done correctly, black espresso streams quickly from the machine, closely followed by the delicious crema. The whole process takes only about twenty-five seconds.

Although some manufacturers offer a relatively inexpensive stovetop version of the espresso machine for $60 to $80, this is not the best solution because you have to keep a close watch. If espresso is your passion, by all means invest in a professional-quality automatic espresso maker, for which you can expect to pay anywhere from $130 to close to $1,000. You'll even find some mid-range machines with a froth dispenser for making authentic cappuccino.

If you sometimes want a cup of regular coffee, sometimes opt for cappuccino or caffè latte, and sometimes prefer an espresso, consider a combination machine that makes both drip coffee and espresso, and includes an instant froth dispenser. You can have it your way for around $200.

Brewing Accessories

As you've seen, some coffee machines come with a range of accessories—for a

A good espresso machine will allow you to make any coffeehouse drink, from a steaming espresso to a chilled caffè freddo. (For details, see page 111.)

price, of course. But if you just aren't ready to take the plunge and buy a plunger pot that brews into a thermal carafe or an espresso maker that has every feature imaginable, there are two handy accessories that will help you better enjoy your coffee-making adventures.

The Thermal Carafe

The warming plates found on electric coffeemakers can turn a good brew bad through overheating. A better option is to decant your fresh-brewed coffee into a thermal carafe, which will maintain the beverage's temperature without making it sour or bitter.

If you're still stuck on your old drip coffeemaker—or you just bought a beautiful new French press—do yourself a great favor and buy a carafe that will hold the coffee at serving temperature for several hours. No more overbrewed, scorched, or stale coffee for you. Thermal carafes are inexpensive. Unless you want to spend $80 to $100 for professional quality, you'll pay only about $20 to $30 for a ten- to twelve-cup carafe.

The Milk Steamer

If you want rich, creamy froth for topping a cappuccino, a caffè latte, or even a plain cup of coffee, consider buying a separate milk steamer. Most of these work by expelling steam through a nozzle, which you insert into a pitcher of cold milk. As the steam mixes with the milk, a creamlike foam is created—a foam that you can easily pour onto the beverage of your choice. Prices vary, but you can expect to pay about $50 for a good steamer.

BREWING THE PERFECT POT

You've lovingly selected your coffee beans, and perhaps have even ground them yourself. Your carefully chosen coffeemaker is at the ready. Now all you need do is brew the perfect pot.

While this may sound easy, many people find that their home-brewed coffee never quite meets their expectations. Just like coffee grinding, good coffeemaking may require some experimentation—especially if you're using a new coffee pot or an unfamiliar type of coffee. However, by keeping some basics in mind, you can greatly improve your coffee each and every time you brew a pot.

To begin, carefully read and follow the instructions that came with your coffeemaker. Every manufacturer of brewing equipment takes great care to provide carefully tested instructions for making a terrific cup of coffee. So if the booklet that came with your machine recommends a certain type of filter or a certain grind, by all means, take heed. Then follow the simple guidelines below to insure the best brew.

- Whenever possible, use freshly roasted high-quality beans and grind them to the proper consistency just before brewing.

- Start with fresh cold water. Remember that brewed coffee contains more water than coffee beans, so water quality makes a difference. If your area has good drinkable water, use it, allowing the water to run from the tap for a few seconds before filling the pot. If your tap water is not up to par, avoid any off taste by using bottled spring water. Do not use distilled or softened water.

- Make sure that your coffeemaker is clean. All brewing equipment should be washed after each use with warm, soapy water, and then rinsed well. If not, the coffee oils will build up in the machine, eventually turning rancid and giving your coffee an unpleasant flavor.

- Use the right amount of coffee. A rule of thumb is to add about two level tablespoons of ground coffee—a standard coffee measure—for every six ounces of water. Then adjust the proportions to taste as desired.

- Brew only as much coffee as you, your family, and your guests will consume at a sitting.

Experts agree that a clean coffeemaker is one of the keys to good coffee. When residues are allowed to build up on the pot, your brew is sure to suffer.

■ Before serving, stir the coffee. Heavier oils tend to sink to the bottom of the pot, while coffee brewed at the beginning of a drip cycle is generally stronger than coffee brewed at the end. Stirring will distribute the oils and insure consistency throughout the pot.

■ Serve your coffee as soon as the brewing cycle is complete, and drink the pot dry within thirty minutes. Coffee that sits on a warming plate longer than thirty minutes not only loses a lot of flavor, but also becomes stale, scorched, and bitter.

■ If you wish to preserve the fresh-brewed flavor of your coffee to enjoy later, decant the brew into an insulated carafe as soon as the brewing cycle is complete. When you set the pot to brewing, put very hot water into the carafe and pop on the lid. When the brewing cycle is complete, the thermos will be well warmed and won't steal heat from the brew. Most insulated carafes will keep the coffee hot and fresh-tasting for up to four hours.

Hopefully, the coffee you prepare at home now rivals that of the best coffeehouses, and you are happily sipping it in your kitchen and sharing it with admiring family and friends. But there are so many more ways to enjoy the wonders of the coffee bean! In Part Two, you'll find a wealth of recipes—recipes for specialty drinks like Frosty Mocha Shakes and scrumptious coffee accompaniments like Sweet Currant Scones and buttery croissants. To learn more confessions of the coffee bean, turn the page.

PART TWO

The **Tastes** & **Pleasures** of the **Coffee Bean**

Delectable Coffee **Drinks**

*What would one do
without one's morning coffee?*

—NOEL COWARD (1899–1973)

In Chapter 6, you learned all the basics of brewing a great cup of coffee. But if you're a true coffee lover, you won't want to stop there, because there are so many wonderful beverages you can make with the coffee bean. This chapter explores the wide variety of coffee drinks you can whip up at home—for yourself, for your family, or for your admiring guests.

The chapter begins with a selection of hot coffee drinks that can warm the coldest morning, provide a pick-me-up on a dreary afternoon, or make a perfect ending to a perfect dinner. Whether you prefer a creamy Café au Lait, a decadently rich Brandied Mocha Coffee, or a spicy Mexican Mocha, you'll find a brew to suit your tastes. You'll even be tempted by a recipe for Gild-the-Lily Whipped Cream, which can turn the most humble cup of coffee into a crowd pleaser.

If the summer sun has left you craving a frosty delight, you'll be pleased to find a sampling of chilled coffees, from simple Icy Vanilla Coffee to intense Espresso Shake to sweet and spicy Turkish Delight. If you like your summer drinks a bit more "spirited," don't worry. Frosty Mocha Shake enhances the marriage of coffee and chocolate with a splash of brandy, and egg-enriched Danish Cognackaffee—a chilled cognac-coffee creation—is a dessert in itself.

So don't wait for a visit to your local coffeehouse to savor a steaming latte or a mocha-laced shake. With just a few simple ingredients and a few minutes, you can enjoy these delights and many more in the best coffeehouse of all—your own home.

HOT COFFEE DRINKS

CAFÉ AU LAIT

YIELD: 4 SERVINGS

2 cups freshly brewed French roast coffee

2 cups milk, at room temperature or warmed

Café au Lait is the French version of Caffè Latte. Although cappuccino has almost overtaken it in popularity in the coffee bars of France, café au lait is still what most French people prefer for breakfast.

1. Divide the coffee equally among 4 mugs. Top with an equal amount of the milk and stir.

2. Serve immediately.

Coffeehouse Coffees

If you have invested in an espresso machine, you'll find it a snap to prepare the wonderful espresso drinks that you so enjoy in your favorite coffeehouse. The following definitions of various espresso beverages are in themselves recipes. Prepare each cup individually, just as is done at a coffee bar.

Caffè Americano. Espresso brought to the equivalent of drip coffee by diluting it with hot water.

Caffè Freddo. Chilled, sweetened espresso served in a tall glass, sometimes over ice.

Caffè Latte. Espresso that is well diluted with steamed milk, but without much foam. Usually made with more milk than a cappuccino, the caffè latte is the milder of the two drinks and is a popular breakfast beverage throughout Italy.

Caffè Mocha. One part espresso, one part steamed milk, and one part hot chocolate.

Cappuccino. One part espresso, one part steamed milk, and one part foamed milk. Because there's not much dilution, a cappuccino has more intense coffee flavor than a caffè latte.

Doppio. A double espresso—in other words, about 3 ounces—served in a 5- to 6-ounce cappuccino cup. The cappuccino cup is not filled to the rim with the espresso.

Espresso. A single "shot"—1 to 1 1/2 ounces—of dark, rich coffee, traditionally served in a pre-warmed demitasse cup.

Espresso Con Panna. A single shot of espresso crowned with whipped cream.

Espresso Lungo. A "long" espresso made with the same amount of coffee as a single shot, but with more water. This is sometimes called an Americano.

Espresso Macchiato. A single shot of espresso "marked" or "stained" with a bit of steamed milk.

Espresso Ristretto. Literally, a "short" espresso. An espresso ristretto is made using the same amount of coffee as a regular espresso, but less water—sometimes as little as 1/2 ounce per serving.

Latte Macchiato. Steamed milk "marked" or "stained" with a shot of espresso. This drink is served in a tall glass rather than a cup.

YIELD: 4 SMALL
SERVINGS

½ cup dark-roasted
coffee beans,
powdered*

¼ cup sugar

2 ⅓ cups cold water

*The key to Turkish coffee is
the grind. The beans must be
so finely ground they turn
into a rich black powder.
If you don't grind your own
beans, use the espresso
setting on the grinder at
the market where you
purchase coffee, or simply
buy expresso grind.

MOCK TURKISH COFFEE

*Unless you have an ibrik (see Chapter 6), it's impossible to make
authentic Turkish coffee. However, you can approximate that strong,
sweet brew at home using a saucepan on the top of your stove.
Turkish coffee is served in very small cups, usually without handles.
If you have them, demitasse cups make a good substitute.*

1. Place all the powdered coffee, all the sugar, and 2 cups of the water in a heavy medium-sized saucepan, and stir until the sugar is dissolved.

2. Bring the coffee to a rapid boil over high heat. Remove the pan from the heat, stir the coffee, and allow the grounds to settle.

3. Return the saucepan to the stove and repeat Step 2 three times.

4. Remove the pot from the third boiling, cover, and let sit undisturbed for 2 minutes.

5. Stir the remaining ⅓ cup of cold water into the coffee. Cover and allow the coffee to rest for 1 minute to settle the grounds.

6. To avoid disturbing the grounds, slowly pour the coffee into 4 small cups and serve immediately. Sip slowly and savor every drop.

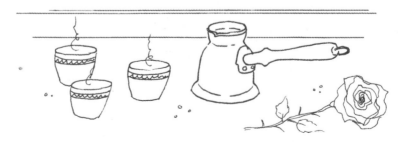

CAFÉ KAHLÚA

This is a White Russian in a cup. If you omit the cream, you can call it a Black Russian. Feel free to use any coffee-flavored liqueur, as all will yield excellent results. Just be aware that this is a potent brew!

1. Place the coffee, liqueur, and vodka in a medium-sized saucepan, and stir to combine. Cook over low heat until very hot, but do allow the mixture to boil.

2. Stir the heavy cream into the coffee, and immediately divide among 4 mugs.

3. Top each cup with whipped cream, if desired, and serve immediately.

YIELD: **4** SERVINGS

2 1/2 cups freshly brewed strong coffee

1/2 cup coffee-flavored liqueur, such as Kahlúa or Tia Maria

1/4 cup vodka

1/2 cup heavy cream

Whipped cream for garnish (optional)

IRISH COFFEE

Without a doubt, Irish coffee is the best-known whiskey-spiked coffee in the world. Select a smooth and mellow Irish whiskey for this irresistible after-dinner delight. This coffee is traditionally served in warmed glass mugs, but any cup or mug will do very well.

1. Prewarm 4 mugs by filling them with hot water. Set aside.

2. Place the heavy cream and powdered sugar in a small mixing bowl, and use an electric mixer to whip the cream until stiff. Refrigerate until needed.

3. Drain the water from the mugs, and divide the coffee equally among them. Place 1 shot (3 tablespoons) of whiskey and sugar to taste in each mug, and stir until the sugar is dissolved.

4. Top each cup with a drift of whipped cream, and serve immediately.

YIELD: **4** SERVINGS

1/2 cup heavy cream

2 tablespoons powdered sugar, sifted

3 cups freshly brewed coffee

4 shots Irish whiskey (3/4 cup)

Sugar to taste

YIELD: 4 SERVINGS

1/2 cup heavy cream

2 tablespoons powdered sugar, sifted

3 cups freshly brewed coffee

4 shots Irish Cream whiskey (3/4 cup)

Sugar to taste

IRISH CREAM COFFEE

Irish Cream is one of the most popular flavored coffees in all forms,
both instant and whole bean. But the real thing is even better.

1. Prewarm 4 mugs by filling them with hot water. Set aside.

2. Place the heavy cream and powdered sugar in a small mixing bowl, and use an electric mixer to whip the cream until stiff. Refrigerate until needed.

3. Drain the water from the mugs, and divide the coffee equally among them. Place 1 shot (3 tablespoons) of Irish Cream whiskey and sugar to taste in each mug, and stir until the sugar is dissolved.

4. Top each cup with a drift of whipped cream, and serve immediately.

YIELD: 4 SERVINGS

1/3 cup chocolate liqueur, such as crème de cacao

1/3 cup brandy

1/3 cup heavy cream, warmed to room temperature

1/4 cup coffee liqueur, such as Kahlúa or Tia Maria

2 cups freshly brewed strong coffee

COFFEE ALEXANDER

If you like an occasional Brandy Alexander,
this delectable cup of coffee is for you.
It is so rich, it's almost decadent.

1. Prewarm 4 mugs by filling them with hot water. Set aside.

2. Place the chocolate liqueur, brandy, heavy cream, and coffee liqueur in a medium-sized bowl, and stir to combine.

3. Drain the water from the mugs, and divide the liqueur mixture equally among them. Fill each cup to the brim with the coffee, and serve immediately.

SPICY PLANTATION COFFEE

YIELD: 4 SERVINGS

*Because it's spiked with rum, this coffee makes me think
of lounging on cushioned wicker on a shaded veranda.
I am facing lush lawns that slope down to a lazy river,
which sparkles in the glow of a glorious sunset.
An elephant trumpets and a lion roars in the distance.
Close your eyes and pretend while you sip.*

1. Place the heavy cream and powdered sugar in a small mixing bowl, and use an electric mixer to whip the cream until stiff. Refrigerate until needed.

2. Place the rum, orange peel, cloves, and sugar in a small saucepan, and cook over low heat, stirring, until the sugar dissolves. Continue cooking until the rum barely reaches a simmer.

3. Remove the saucepan from the heat, cover, and let steep for at least 5 minutes to allow the flavors to meld.

4. Return the saucepan to the heat, whisk in the coffee, and bring to a simmer.

5. Divide the coffee equally among 4 mugs, pouring it through a tea strainer. Top each with a drift of whipped cream and a sprinkling of nutmeg, and serve immediately.

½ cup heavy cream

2 tablespoons powdered sugar, sifted

4 shots dark rum (¾ cup)

4 thin strips orange peel, cut in half

8 whole cloves

4 teaspoons sugar, or to taste

3 cups freshly brewed strong coffee

Grated nutmeg for garnish

YIELD: **4 SERVINGS**

1 ⅓ cups whole milk

2 cinnamon sticks, broken into thirds

15 whole cloves

¾ teaspoon aniseed

3 ½ ounces semisweet chocolate, shaved

1 ½ tablespoons brown sugar, packed

2 cups freshly brewed coffee

¼ cup coffee liqueur, such as Kahlúa or Tia Maria (optional)

MEXICAN MOCHA

If you are able to find sweet and spicy cinnamon-spiked Mexican chocolate, use it in place of the semisweet chocolate, brown sugar, and cinnamon called for in this recipe. If not, the ingredients used below will allow you to enjoy authentic Mexican flavor.

1. Place the milk, cinnamon sticks, cloves, and aniseed in a large heavy saucepan, and bring to a simmer over medium heat, stirring occasionally. Add the chocolate and brown sugar, and stir until the chocolate is melted and the sugar is dissolved.

2. Remove the saucepan from the heat, cover, and let steep for 30 to 40 minutes to allow the flavors to meld.

3. Return the saucepan to the heat, whisk in the coffee, and bring to a simmer.

4. If using the liqueur, place 1 tablespoon in each of 4 mugs. Divide the coffee equally among the mugs, pouring it through a tea strainer, and serve immediately.

MOCHA DELIGHT

YIELD: **4** SERVINGS

*I don't think there's a better pairing of flavors than chocolate and coffee.
It's an especially good match when freshly brewed coffee
is mated with chocolate and coffee liqueurs.*

½ cup heavy cream

2 tablespoons
powdered sugar, sifted

1. Place the heavy cream and powdered sugar in a small mixing bowl, and use an electric mixer to whip the cream until stiff. Refrigerate until needed.

⅓ cup coffee liqueur, such as Kahlúa or Tia Maria

2. Place the liqueurs in a small bowl, and stir to combine.

⅓ cup chocolate liqueur, such as crème de cacao

3. Divide the liqueur mixture equally among 4 mugs. Then fill each cup to the brim with the coffee.

3 cups freshly brewed strong coffee

4. Top each cup with a drift of whipped cream, and serve immediately.

BRANDIED MOCHA COFFEE

YIELD: **4** SERVINGS

This Viennese-style mocha is enriched with brandy.

¾ cup heavy cream, divided

1. Place ½ cup of the heavy cream and all of the powdered sugar in a small mixing bowl, and use an electric mixer to whip the cream until stiff. Refrigerate until needed.

2 tablespoons
powdered sugar, sifted

4 ounces semisweet chocolate, shaved

2. Place the remaining cream in a large heavy saucepan, and cook over low heat until it barely comes to a simmer. Add the chocolate and cook, stirring constantly, until the chocolate is melted. Slowly whisk in the coffee and the brandy.

3½ cups freshly brewed coffee

⅓ cup brandy

3. Divide the mixture equally among 4 mugs. Top each with a drift of whipped cream and a dusting of cinnamon, and serve immediately.

Ground cinnamon for garnish

YIELD: **4** SERVINGS

¾ cup heavy cream, divided

2 tablespoons powdered sugar, sifted

4 ounces semisweet chocolate, shaved

4 cups freshly brewed coffee

Ground cinnamon for garnish

VIENNESE-STYLE MOCHA COFFEE

This delightful variation on the chocolate-coffee theme is minus the liqueurs, so feel free to serve it to the teetotalers in your life.

1. Place ½ cup of the heavy cream and all of the powdered sugar in a small mixing bowl, and use an electric mixer to whip the cream until stiff. Refrigerate until needed.

2. Place the remaining cream in a large heavy saucepan, and cook over low heat until it barely comes to a simmer. Add the chocolate and cook, stirring constantly, until the chocolate is melted. Slowly whisk in the coffee.

3. Divide the mixture equally among 4 mugs. Top each with a drift of whipped cream and a dusting of cinnamon, and serve immediately.

YIELD:
4 DEMITASSE SERVINGS

2 cups freshly brewed strong coffee

4 tablespoons brandy

4 sugar cubes

CAFÉ ROYALE

Although it's served in demitasse cups, Café Royale isn't as fancy as Café Brulot (see page 120), but the preparation is still a bit of a spectacle in its own right. Add sugar cubes to your shopping list right now.

1. Divide the coffee equally among 4 demitasse cups. Have a demitasse spoon resting in the saucer. It will be needed to stir in the sugar cube.

2. Have the brandy ready in a small pitcher. Balance a tablespoon over a cup and fill the spoon with brandy. Add a sugar cube. Set alight.

3. When the flames lessen, tip the spoon and let the brandy and sugar cube slide into the coffee. Serve immediately.

SOUTH-OF-THE-BORDER COFFEE

YIELD: 4 SERVINGS

*Sweet and hot, this is just the thing to top off a fine meal
on a cold winter's night. Hand each guest a mug and
invite them to join you in front of a roaring fire.*

¹/₂ cup heavy cream

2 tablespoons powdered sugar, sifted

1. Place the heavy cream and powdered sugar in a small mixing bowl, and use an electric mixer to whip the cream until stiff. Refrigerate until needed.

³/₄ cup coffee liqueur, such as Kahlúa or Tia Maria

2. Divide the liqueur evenly among 4 mugs. Add 1 teaspoon of brown sugar to each, and stir to dissolve the sugar.

4 teaspoons dark brown sugar

3. Divide the coffee equally among the mugs, and stir to blend. Top each with a drift of whipped cream and a dusting of cinnamon, and serve immediately.

3 cups freshly brewed coffee

Ground cinnamon for garnish

DREAMY COFFEE

YIELD: 4 SERVINGS

*Any of the recipes in this chapter can be transformed into "sweet dreams"
coffees by using your favorite decaf. But with a splash of liqueur and a
dash of whiskey, this potion will send you off to dreamland in no time.*

4 cups freshly brewed decaffeinated coffee

1. Prewarm 4 mugs by filling them with hot water, and allow to sit for 1 minute. Then drain the water from the mugs and immediately divide the coffee among them.

4 shots (³/₄ cup) coffee liqueur, such as Kahlúa or Tia Maria

4 shots (³/₄ cup) Irish whiskey

2. Place 1 shot (3 tablespoons) each of the liqueur and whiskey in each mug. Stir in sugar and cream to taste, if desired, and serve immediately.

Sugar to taste (optional)

Cream to taste (optional)

YIELD:
4 DEMITASSE SERVINGS

Peel of 1 orange

3 cinnamon sticks

8 whole cloves

4 sugar cubes or
2 tablespoons sugar

⅓ cup brandy

2 cups freshly brewed
coffee

CAFÉ BRULOT

This French-inspired after-dinner coffee is traditionally
flamed tableside on a serving cart and served in demitasse cups.
If the butler is busy with something else, by all means do it yourself.

1. Place the orange peel, cinnamon sticks, cloves, and sugar in a large flame-proof bowl (silver is traditional). Pour the brandy over all and flame by tipping the bowl and waving a flame close to the tipped edge. You don't have to actually touch a flame to the brandy; the fumes will draw down the fire. Allow the flames to die of their own accord.

2. With your best silver ladle or large spoon, stir the brandy mixture to be sure the sugar has dissolved. Slowly add the fresh-brewed coffee.

3. Ladle the mixture into demitasse cups and serve.

YIELD: 4 SERVINGS

3 cups cold water

½ cup ground coffee

UPDATED COWBOY COFFEE

If the time comes when your coffee pot is out of commission, you may
want to know how to brew coffee in a saucepan. Today we know that
cooking coffee at too high a temperature results in a bitter beverage.
I think coffee was given the name "mud" when those old-time cowboys
boiled their coffee and ended up with a thick and cloudy brew.
No matter what method you're using, the water should barely simmer.

1. Place the water in a medium-sized saucepan, and place over high heat just until tiny bubbles appear around the edge of the pot. Remove from the heat and add the coffee, stirring to mix.

The Crowning Touch

Many of the coffee drinks in this chapter are crowned with lightly sweetened whipped cream, adding a touch of velvety sweetness to each of the beverages. If you want to create a real sensation, though, replace the sweetened cream with the following topping. Laced with orange liqueur, Gild-the-Lily Whipped Cream can turn even a plain cup of Joe into a rich indulgence.

GILD-THE-LILY WHIPPED CREAM

2 cups heavy cream

¼ cup orange liqueur,
such as Cointreau

2 tablespoons powdered sugar, sifted

1. Place the heavy cream in a small mixing bowl, and whip the cream with an electric mixer until soft peaks form.

2. Add both the orange liqueur and powdered sugar to the cream, and continue whipping until the flavors are combined and the cream is firm.

3. Cover the bowl with plastic wrap or aluminum foil and refrigerate until needed.

2. Cover the saucepan and allow it to sit undisturbed for 4 to 6 minutes to develop the flavor.

3. Divide the coffee equally among 4 cups, pouring it through a tea strainer, and serve immediately.

COLD COFFEE DRINKS

1/3 cup ground coffee

4 cups water

4–8 Coffee Ice Cubes
(below)

ICED COFFEE

Those who know suggest using finely ground dark-roast beans for coffees that are served with ice, so that additions such as cream and sugar won't dilute the flavor. The amounts given at left will result in a strong brew.

1. Using the coffee and water, brew as your coffeemaker requires.

2. Allow the coffee to cool to room temperature. Use within 2 hours, or cover and refrigerate until needed.

3. Divide the coffee evenly among 4 tall glasses. Drop in the ice cubes, add straws, and serve.

Coffee Ice Cubes

Iced coffee is a wonderful creation, allowing you to enjoy rich coffee flavor on even the hottest of days. The trouble has always been that melting ice cubes dilute the brew, robbing it of flavor. The solution? Instead of using water to make your next tray of ice cubes, fill the tray with coffee!

To make Coffee Ice Cubes, brew a small amount of coffee—a little over a cup—and allow it to cool to room temperature. You may sweeten the coffee or not, depending on which iced delight you will be serving. Then pour the coffee into the ice cube tray, freeze, and use the cubes to chill plain iced coffee or any chilled coffee beverage. This is an especially nice touch if you're carrying a pitcher of summertime coffee out to enjoy poolside or on the deck or patio, or if you're toting iced coffee to a picnic in the park.

For a delightful crunch, add a chocolate-covered roasted coffee bean to each little cubical in the ice tray. But don't keep it a secret! Be sure to tell your guests so that nobody swallows one by mistake.

TURKISH DELIGHT

*Sweet, spicy, and very rich, this icy delight will not be forgotten.
Best of all, you don't need an ibrik—the special pot
used to brew Turkish coffee—to whip it up.*

1. Stir the Simple Syrup or sugar into the hot coffee. Cover and refrigerate until chilled.

2. Place the milk in a small saucepan. Stir in the crushed cardamom pods, and bring to a simmer over medium-high heat, stirring occasionally. Allow to simmer for 5 minutes.

3. Remove the milk from the heat, and pour through a strainer into a pitcher. Stir in the cream and the chilled coffee, and refrigerate until cold.

4. Divide the mixture evenly among 4 tall glasses. Drop in a few Coffee Ice Cubes (page 122) if desired, add straws, and serve.

YIELD: 4 SERVINGS

2 tablespoons Simple Syrup (page 126) or sugar

2 cups freshly brewed dark roast coffee

1 cup milk

8 cardamom pods, crushed

1 cup cream

ICY VANILLA COFFEE

*You'll be surprised at what a touch of vanilla can do for coffee.
This one may become your favorite summertime refresher.*

1. Stir the Simple Syrup or sugar into the hot coffee. Cover and refrigerate until chilled.

2. Stir the vanilla into the cold coffee, and divide evenly among 4 tall glasses. Drop in a few Coffee Ice Cubes (page 122) if desired, add straws, and serve.

YIELD: 4 SERVINGS

2 tablespoons Simple Syrup (page 126) or sugar

4 cups freshly brewed coffee

1/2 teaspoon vanilla extract

THE ESPRESSO SHAKE

YIELD: 4 SERVINGS

4 teaspoons Simple Syrup (page 126) or sugar (optional)

2 cups freshly brewed espresso or dark roast coffee

6–8 Coffee Ice Cubes (page 122)

As you might expect, this shake is very dark and rich,
with intense coffee flavor. If you have an espresso machine,
by all means use it. If not, brew a dark roast at double strength.

1. If using sweetener, stir the Simple Syrup or sugar into the hot coffee. Cover and refrigerate until chilled.

2. Place the Coffee Ice Cubes in a blender, and whirl briefly to crack the ice. Add the chilled coffee and whirl until frothy.

3. Divide the mixture evenly among 4 tall glasses, add straws, and serve.

DANISH COGNACKAFFE

YIELD: 4 SERVINGS

2 cups freshly brewed coffee

3/4 cup egg substitute

1/3 cup sugar

3/4 cup cognac

The name says it all. This is chilled cognac-coffee, made rich with the
addition of eggs. However, the whole eggs in the original recipe have been
replaced with egg substitute, which is safe to use even when uncooked.

1. Cover the coffee and refrigerate until chilled.

2. When the coffee is cold, place the egg substitute in a large mixing bowl and beat with an electric mixer until frothy. Gradually add the sugar, beating continually until the mixture is thick and pale.

3. Slowly stir the cold coffee into the egg mixture, and blend thoroughly. Stir in the cognac, and blend thoroughly. Cover and refrigerate until chilled.

4. Divide the mixture evenly among 4 tall glasses, add straws, and serve.

THE CAPPUCCINO PITCHER

YIELD: **4** SERVINGS

*If your crowd loves cappuccino, an icy pitcherful will be welcome
at your next outdoor gathering. Sweeten it or not,
depending on the preference of your guests.*

1. If using sweetener, stir the Simple Syrup or sugar into the hot coffee. Cover and refrigerate until chilled.

2. Transfer the cold coffee to your best pitcher and stir in the cold milk.

3. To serve, pour into tall glasses, adding a few Coffee Ice Cubes (page 122) if desired. If you like, sprinkle each glassful with a little cinnamon, and add a straw as you serve.

2 tablespoons Simple Syrup (page 126) or sugar (optional)

4 cups freshly brewed espresso or dark roast coffee

1/2 cup milk, chilled

Ground cinnamon for garnish (optional)

PLANTATION PUNCH

YIELD: **4** SERVINGS

*Dessert in a glass is the best way to describe
this frothy coffee confection.*

1. Cover the coffee and refrigerate until chilled.

2. Place 1 cup of the cold coffee in a blender. Add the ice cream and rum, and blend well. Add the remaining coffee, and blend until frothy.

3. Taste to correct the flavorings. If you want a sweeter drink, add the Simple Syrup.

4. Divide the mixture evenly among 4 tall glasses. Drop in a few Coffee Ice Cubes (page 122) if desired, add straws, and serve.

4 cups freshly brewed strong coffee

1 quart coffee or vanilla ice cream, softened

1 cup rum

1/4 cup Simple Syrup (page 126) (optional)

A Simple Solution

Just about everyone has had the experience of stirring granulated sugar into a chilled drink and watching the crystals fall to the bottom of the glass, where they stubbornly refuse to dissolve. The result is an unsweetened drink that ends with an unpleasant mouthful of sugar granules.

Fortunately, the solution to this problem is simple. Simple Syrup—a cooked mixture of sugar and water—is a snap to make, and can be easily stirred into the iciest of drinks. Make this syrup at the beginning of the summer and enjoy sweet iced coffee all season long.

SIMPLE SYRUP

YIELD: ABOUT 1 CUP

1 cup sugar

1 cup water

1. Place the sugar and water in a large heavy saucepan, and cook over low heat, stirring occasionally, until the mixture reaches a simmer. Continue to cook at a simmer, stirring occasionally, for about 5 minutes, or until all of the sugar crystals are completely dissolved.

2. Allow the mixture to cool completely. Then pour into a glass jar with a tight lid and store in the refrigerator until needed. Simple Syrup keeps indefinitely.

FROSTY MOCHA SHAKE

*I hate to repeat myself, but coffee and chocolate
is such a marvelous marriage of flavors
that it continues to be a personal favorite.*

1. Cool the coffee to room temperature and pour into 2 ice cube trays. Freeze until solid.

2. Pop the cubes out of the trays and place them in a blender with all of the remaining ingredients. Blend until frothy.

3. Divide the mixture evenly among 4 tall glasses, add straws, and serve.

YIELD: 4 SERVINGS

2 cups freshly brewed strong coffee

2 cups cold milk

$1/2$–1 cup chocolate syrup

$1/4$ cup brandy

KAHLÚA AND CREAM SHAKE

*Words fail me. This is indescribably creamy,
delicious, and delectable.*

1. Cover the coffee and refrigerate until chilled.

2. Place the cold coffee, ice cream, and liqueur in a blender, and blend until frothy.

3. Divide the mixture evenly among 4 tall glasses. Drop in a few Coffee Ice Cubes (page 122) if desired, add straws, and serve.

YIELD: 4 SERVINGS

4 cups freshly brewed coffee

4 scoops vanilla ice cream (about 1 cup)

$3/4$ cup coffee liqueur, such as Kahlúa or Tia Maria

CHAPTER 7

Scrumptious Coffee Accompaniments

*The morning cup of coffee has an exhilaration about it
which the cheering influence of the afternoon or evening cup of tea
cannot be expected to reproduce.*

—OLIVER WENDELL HOLMES (1809–1894)

Although a cup of good coffee is a reward in itself, the experience is made all the more pleasurable when your cappuccino or espresso is accompanied by a savory bread or a lusciously sweet dessert. This chapter presents a wide range of companions for your coffee, from satisfying coffeecakes to buttery croissants to crisp biscotti to creamy puddings and custards. For good measure, I've even thrown in a few not-to-be-missed candies.

While every creation in this chapter is a great coffee companion, quite a few also use coffee as a flavoring. Creamy Coffee Cheesecake, for instance, unites prepared coffee with Kahlúa liqueur for a double coffee punch. And, of course, roasted coffee beans are an essential ingredient in chocolate-drenched Coffee Bean Clusters. To prevent caffeine overload, consider using decaffeinated coffee in these treats, especially if you're accompanying them with a cup of coffee. That way, you'll be able to enjoy a delicious dessert without sacrificing a good night's sleep. And if you have no leftover coffee on hand to use as flavoring, and you don't feel like brewing a pot, try stirring up some instant coffee. In fact, although you might not choose to drink it, superstrong instant is a great means of injecting coffee flavor into baked goods.

You'll be glad to know that all of the tempting creations presented in this chapter were kitchen tested and tasted until the results were just right. So the next time your cup of Joe looks a little lonely, pair it with one of the following homemade treats. Your coffee beans will thank you.

CAKES AND PIES

APPLE-CRUNCH COFFEECAKE

Like the Rich and Quick Sour Cream Coffeecake on page 141,
this one is quickly made. The recipe calls for apples,
but you may substitute peaches if that's your pleasure.

1. To make the topping, place the brown sugar, wheat germ, and nuts in a small bowl, and stir to combine. Set aside.

2. To make the batter, place the flours, sugar, baking soda, cinnamon, and nutmeg in a large bowl, and stir well to combine. Set aside.

3. Peel and core the apples, and slice them very thinly. You should have about 2 1/2 cups. Set aside.

4. Place the egg in a small bowl, and beat until frothy. Stir the egg, apple juice, and sour cream into the dry ingredients. Fold in the apples and raisins.

5. Lightly grease a 9-inch round cake pan, or coat lightly with cooking spray. Pour the batter into the pan, and evenly sprinkle with the topping.

6. Bake in a preheated 350°F oven for about 30 minutes, or until a toothpick inserted in the center comes out clean.

7. Place the pan on a wire rack, and allow to cool completely. Cut into wedges and serve.

YIELD: 9-INCH CAKE

BATTER

1 1/2 cups all purpose flour

1/2 cup whole wheat flour

1/2 cup sugar

1 teaspoon baking soda

1/2 teaspoon ground cinnamon

1/4 teaspoon ground nutmeg

3 apples

1 egg

1/2 cup apple juice

1/4 cup sour cream

1/4 cup dark or golden raisins

TOPPING

2 tablespoons brown sugar

2 tablespoons wheat germ

2 tablespoons finely chopped walnuts

YIELD: 8-INCH TORTE

BATTER

½ cup (1 stick) butter, softened

⅔ cup powdered sugar

4 ounces German sweet chocolate

6 eggs

1 heaping cup plain bread crumbs

1 teaspoon ground cinnamon

½ teaspoon ground cloves

¼ teaspoon salt

FILLING

1 jar (18 ounces) apricot jam

CHOCOLATE GLAZE

4 ounces German sweet chocolate

2 tablespoons butter

SACHER TORTE

A selection of Austrian desserts is always tantalizing.
Although I always want a little bit of everything,
I can never resist Austria's renowned Sacher Torte.

1. To make the batter, place the butter in a medium-sized bowl and cream with an electric mixer until very soft. Sift the powdered sugar and beat it into the butter gradually.

2. To melt the chocolate, place it in a microwave-safe dish and heat it on high for 10 to 15 seconds. Alternatively, heat in a double boiler until melted. Add to the butter mixture and beat in.

3. Separate the eggs one at a time. Beat one yolk at a time into the batter, placing the whites in a separate medium-sized bowl as you go along.

4. Make sure the bread crumbs are finely crushed. If not, use a rolling pin or food processor to crush further. Beat the crumbs, cinnamon, and cloves into the batter.

5. Add the salt to the egg whites and beat with the electric mixer until stiff peaks form. Fold the beaten whites into the batter.

6. Lightly grease two 8-inch round cake pans, or coat lightly with cooking spray. Divide the batter between the pans and bake in a preheated 350°F oven for 20 to 25 minutes, or until a toothpick inserted in the center comes out clean.

7. Cool for about 10 minutes before removing the cakes from the pans. Allow the layers to cool completely on a wire rack.

8. Divide each of the cooled cake layers in half horizontally. To get a clean cut, break off about a 24-inch length of sewing thread. Make a small slit on one side of the cake, and use the thread to "saw" your way through the layer, keeping the thread centered in the outside edge of the layer. When you're almost through, cross the ends of the thread over and pull slowly until the thread comes out. Repeat with the other layer.

9. If the jam is stiff, stir it until it is soft enough to spread without tearing the cake.

10. Lift off the cut top of 1 layer and place it cut-side up on a serving plate. Spread with a third of the jam. Place the bottom half of the cut layer on top of the filling cut-side up, and spread with a third of the jam. Continue assembling the torte, ending with the final layer cut-side down to make a smooth surface for the chocolate glaze.

11. To make the glaze, place the chocolate and butter in a small microwave-safe bowl, and heat on high for 15 to 20 seconds, or until melted. Alternatively, heat in a double boiler until melted. Stir until the chocolate and butter are well blended.

12. Spread the glaze over the top of the cake. Welcome any drips that run down the sides, smoothing them with the blade of a knife, if you wish. Allow the glaze to set for about 20 minutes before serving.

YIELD: 8-INCH CAKE

DECADENT CHOCOLATE-JAM CAKE

*This rich flourless cake tastes like something you might find
on a dessert cart in an elegant Austrian restaurant.
Although truly delectable and impressive,
it is quite easy to make.*

YIELD: 8-INCH CAKE

BATTER

7 ounces (³⁄₄ cup plus 2 tablespoons) ground almonds

4 eggs

6 ounces German sweet chocolate

¹⁄₂ cup (1 stick) butter, at room temperature

¹⁄₂ cup sugar

TOPPING

1 jar (10 ounces) jam of any flavor (raspberry, apricot, and orange marmalade are all good choices)

CHOCOLATE GLAZE

4 ounces German sweet chocolate

2 tablespoons butter

1. If you haven't been able to find ground almonds, grind them in a nut grinder or whirl them in a food processor or blender until you have fine-ground almond meal. Set aside.

2. Separate the eggs, placing the yolks in a small bowl and the whites in a medium-sized mixing bowl. Using an electric mixer, beat the whites until stiff, and set aside.

3. To melt the chocolate, place it in a microwave-safe dish and heat it on high for 20 to 30 seconds. Alternatively, heat in a double boiler until melted. Set aside.

4. Place the butter in a large bowl, and cream with an electric mixer until very soft. Add the sugar, and continue beating until the mixture is light and fluffy.

5. Beat the egg yolks and melted chocolate into the butter. Beat in the ground almonds.

6. Fold the egg whites gently into the batter, and stir just until blended.

7. Lightly grease an 8-inch round cake pan, or coat lightly with cooking spray. Pour the batter into the pan, smoothing the top with a knife, and bake in a preheated 350°F oven for about 20 minutes, or until a toothpick inserted in the center comes out clean. Don't overbake this tender cake.

8. Allow the cake to cool in the pan for about 5 minutes. Then turn the pan upside down, turning the cake onto a serving plate. Allow to cool completely.

9. If the jam is stiff, stir it until soft enough to spread without tearing the cake. Spread the entire jar of jam over the top of the cake.

10. To make the glaze, place the chocolate and butter in a small microwave-safe bowl, and heat on high for 15 to 20 seconds, or until melted. Alternatively, heat in a double boiler until melted. Stir until the chocolate and butter are well blended.

11. Use a light hand to spread the chocolate over the jam. Welcome any drips that run down the sides, smoothing them with the blade of a knife, if you wish. Allow the glaze to set for about 20 minutes before serving.

YIELD: 9-INCH CAKE

FILLING

2 cans (15 1/4 ounces each) unsweetened cherries

1/3 cup sugar

1/4 teaspoon almond extract (optional)

2 tablespoons cold water

1 1/2 tablespoons cornstarch

CRUST

1 1/2 cups all purpose flour

1/3 cup sugar

1 1/2 teaspoons ground cinnamon

1/8 teaspoon salt

1/2 cup butter (1 stick), softened

1 egg, beaten to a froth

SOUR CREAM CHERRY CAKE

*My mother-in-law was a cook of the old school—she never used a recipe.
But this luscious cherry cake is much like the ones I remember
her preparing and serving. Although Gramma Antol
called it a cake, it is more like a fruit tart.*

1. Drain the cherries well, reserving the juice. Place the drained cherries in a small mixing bowl, and sprinkle with the sugar. Set the cherries aside to draw out the juices.

2. While the cherries are "juicing," prepare the crust by sifting the flour, sugar, cinnamon, and salt together into a medium-sized mixing bowl. Rub the butter in or cut it in with 2 knives until the mixture is crumbly and forms pieces the size of peas.

3. Add the beaten egg to the crust mixture, and incorporate as best you can with a fork. Using your hands, lightly work the dough just until it holds together. If very soft, refrigerate for 30 minutes.

4. Pat the dough evenly into a 9-inch pan, making sure the crust comes up the sides. (I use a glass pie plate and it works very well). Refrigerate the unbaked crust until the filling is ready.

5. To complete the filling, drain the sugared cherries and measure the juice. You should have 3/4 cup. If not, add the reserved cherry juice as needed. Transfer the cherry juice to a small saucepan, and place over low heat. Stir in the almond extract, if desired.

6. Place the cold water and cornstarch in a small dish, and stir until dissolved. Stir the cornstarch mixture into the cherry juice mixture.

7. Bring the cherry juice mixture to a simmer, stirring constantly, and allow to simmer until the mixture is slightly thickened. Continue cooking, still stirring, for 3 to 5 minutes, or until the filling becomes clear.

8. Add the cherries to the juice mixture, and stir to combine. Remove the saucepan from the heat and cool for about 30 minutes, or until the mixture is lukewarm.

9. Pour the filling evenly into the cold crust, and bake in a preheated 350°F oven for about 40 minutes, or until the crust is lightly browned. Cool on a wire rack.

10. To make the sour cream topping, stir all the topping ingredients together in a small bowl. Refrigerate until ready to serve.

11. When the cake has cooled a bit, but is still warm, cut into wedges. Top each wedge with a generous dollop of the sour cream topping and serve.

TOPPING

1 cup sour cream

1 tablespoon sugar

$\frac{1}{4}$ teaspoon vanilla extract

OLD-FASHIONED COFFEECAKE WREATH

*Serve this classic wreath for dessert
or for a superlative Sunday morning breakfast.*

SPONGE

1/2 cup lukewarm water

I package (1/2 ounce) dry yeast

I tablespoon sugar

1/2 cup all purpose flour

DOUGH

1/2 cup (I stick) butter, softened

1/4 cup sugar

1/2 teaspoon salt

2 eggs

1 3/4 cups all purpose flour

1. To make the sponge, place the lukewarm water in a medium-sized bowl. Add the dry yeast and sugar, and stir to dissolve. Sift in the 1/2 cup flour, stirring well to combine. Cover and set aside in a warm place for about 30 minutes, or until light and full of bubbles.

2. To make the dough, place the butter in a large bowl, and cream with an electric mixer until very soft. Add the sugar gradually, beating until light.

3. Beat in the salt and eggs, one at a time, until well blended. Beat in the sponge until thoroughly combined.

4. Gradually add the flour to the dough, beating continually. If the dough gets too stiff to work, use a dough hook or your hands to incorporate the rest of the flour.

5. Turn the dough onto a lightly floured board, and knead until the dough is smooth and elastic.

6. Place the dough in a large, clean, lightly greased bowl. Cover and put in a warm place for 2 hours, or until the dough has doubled in size.

7. Place the dough on a lightly floured board, and use a rolling pin to roll it into a 9-x-14-inch rectangle.

8. To fill the wreath, first spread the dough with the softened butter. Then place the sugars and cinnamon in a small bowl, stir to combine, and sprinkle evenly over the butter. Sprinkle on the raisins and the citron and nuts, if desired.

9. Starting at the long side, roll the dough into a log, pressing lightly as you go to encourage the filling to stay in place.

10. Lightly grease a large baking sheet, or coat lightly with cooking spray. Transfer the log to the sheet and gently bring the two ends together to form a circular wreath. Moisten the edges with water and press together well to seal.

11. Dust a sharp serrated knife or kitchen scissors with flour, and cut slits around the outside circumference of the ring. The cuts should be spaced about $1\frac{1}{2}$ inches apart at the outside edge, and taper to about $\frac{1}{2}$ inch apart toward the center. End the cuts about 1 inch from the center, being careful not to cut the wreath all the way through. Tip each slice slightly to the side as you work. Cover lightly and allow to rise in a warm place for 30 to 40 minutes, or until doubled in size.

12. Bake in a preheated 350°F oven for 25 to 30 minutes, or until lightly browned. Let the pan rest on a wire rack while you make the glaze.

13. To make the glaze, place the powdered sugar, hot water, and vanilla extract in a small microwave-safe bowl, and stir until smooth. Drop in the butter.

14. To eliminate the raw taste of the uncooked powdered sugar, place the icing in a microwave oven, and heat on high for 20 seconds, or until the butter melts. Alternatively, place the mixture in a small saucepan, and cook over low heat, stirring constantly, for 1 minute.

15. Drizzle the glaze over the warm wreath, smoothing with a knife, if you wish. Serve.

FILLING

$\frac{1}{4}$ cup ($\frac{1}{2}$ stick) butter, well softened

$\frac{1}{8}$ cup sugar

$\frac{1}{8}$ cup brown sugar

2 teaspoons ground cinnamon

$\frac{1}{2}$ cup dark or golden raisins

$\frac{1}{4}$ cup chopped citron (optional)

$\frac{1}{4}$ cup chopped walnuts (optional)

GLAZE

1 cup powdered sugar

$1\frac{1}{2}$ tablespoons hot water

$\frac{1}{4}$ teaspoon vanilla extract

1 tablespoon butter, softened

LAZY DAY PEACH PIE

YIELD: 8-INCH PIE

2 cans (15¼ ounces each) sliced Freestone (not Cling) peaches

¼ cup sugar

¼ teaspoon ground cinnamon (optional)

⅛ teaspoon ground nutmeg (optional)

I tablespoon cornstarch

I tablespoon cold water

Frozen pastry for a double-crust 8-inch pie

Sugar

This pie relies on canned peaches, which makes it quick and easy, yet still delicious. The added advantage is that the peaches are always soft, never hard and undercooked, which can be a problem with a peach pie that starts with whole fruit. I prefer a pure, unflavored peach filling, but add the spices if you like.

1. Drain the peaches, reserving the juice. You should have about 1 cup of juice. If necessary, add water to reach the desired amount. Set the peach slices aside.

2. Place the juice in a small saucepan over low heat. Stir in the sugar and the spices, if desired.

3. Dissolve the cornstarch in the cold water, and stir into the juice mixture. Cook, stirring constantly, until the sugar is dissolved and the juice thickens and becomes clear.

4. Arrange the drained peaches in a pie pan covered with an uncooked bottom crust. Pour the hot juice over the peaches, and cover with the top crust. Slit in several places and sprinkle with the sugar.

5. Place the pie in a preheated 450°F oven, and bake for 15 minutes. Reduce the temperature to 350°F without opening the oven, and continue baking for 40 to 50 minutes, or until the crust is lightly browned.

6. Transfer the pie to a wire rack, and cool either partially or completely. Serve warm or at room temperature.

RICH AND QUICK SOUR CREAM COFFEECAKE

YIELD: 9-INCH CAKE

Because this coffeecake uses baking powder rather than yeast as leavening, it goes right into the oven as soon as the batter is finished. Note that it is best to make the crumb topping first so there's no delay when the batter is ready for the oven.

1. To make the topping, place all of the topping ingredients in a food processor, and pulse until the butter is incorporated. Stop when you have achieved a crumbly texture, and set aside. Alternatively, mix the dry ingredients together in a medium-sized bowl, and cut the butter in with 2 knives or a pastry cutter until the mixture is crumbly.

2. To make the batter, place the eggs in a medium-sized mixing bowl, and beat with an electric mixer until frothy. Add the sour cream, and beat until combined. Then beat in the sugar.

3. Sift the flour, baking powder, baking soda, and salt into a medium-sized bowl. Gradually beat the dry ingredients into the egg mixture until well blended.

4. Lightly grease a 9-inch round cake pan, or coat lightly with cooking spray. Pour the batter into the pan, and evenly sprinkle with the crumb topping.

5. Bake in a preheated 350°F oven for 18 to 20 minutes, or until a toothpick inserted in the center comes out clean.

6. Place the pan on a wire rack, and cool for at least 30 minutes. (Note that this coffeecake is very tender and won't cut well when hot.) Cut into wedges and serve.

BATTER

2 eggs

1 cup sour cream

1 cup sugar

1 1/2 cups all purpose flour

2 teaspoons baking powder

1/2 teaspoon baking soda

1/4 teaspoon salt

CRUMB TOPPING

1/2 cup all purpose flour

1/4 cup brown sugar, packed

1/4 cup sugar

3 tablespoons cold butter, cut into pieces

CREAMY COFFEE CHEESECAKE

If you like flavored cheesecakes, you'll find this one superlative—
on a par with the best you've ever had.

1. To prepare the crust, place all of the crust ingredients in a medium-sized bowl, and toss with a fork or mix with your hands until well blended.

2. Place the crust mixture in a 9-inch springform pan or a deep dish pie pan. Using the back of a spoon or your hands, press the crumbs firmly around the bottom and sides of the pan. Refrigerate the crust for at least 1 hour, or until very cold.

3. To make the filling, place the cream cheese in a large mixing bowl, and beat with an electric mixer until very soft. Add the sugar, and beat into the cream cheese.

4. Dissolve the instant coffee in the hot water, and beat into the cream cheese mixture. Then beat in the eggs, one at a time, until well blended.

5. Add the sour cream and the liqueur, if desired, to the filling, and beat slowly until thoroughly combined.

6. Pour the filling into the chilled crust and bake in a preheated 350°F oven for 40 minutes, or until the filling is set and a knife inserted in the center comes out clean.

7. Place the pan on a wire rack, and cool for 40 to 60 minutes, or until the cake reaches room temperature.

8. To make the topping, place the sour cream in a medium-sized mixing bowl, and gently stir in the remaining ingredients. When well blended, spread the topping over the cooled cheesecake.

9. Bake the topped cheesecake in a preheated 425°F oven for 5 minutes, or just long enough to set the sour cream. Allow to cool on a wire rack. Refrigerate for at least 4 hours before cutting into wedges and serving.

POPPY SEED COFFEECAKE WREATH

YIELD: 9-INCH WREATH

My mother-in-law, a superlative cook, produced delectable coffeecakes. I was always especially enamored of her poppy seed-filled pastries. If you feel the same way, try this variation of the Old-Fashioned Coffeecake Wreath presented on page 138.

1 recipe Old-Fashioned Coffeecake Wreath (page 138) minus filling

FILLING

½ cup poppy seeds

¼ cup milk

¼ cup sugar

½ teaspoon vanilla extract

1 egg

1. To make the filling, place the poppy seeds and milk in a small bowl, and stir to mix. Allow the seeds to soften in the milk for 2 hours.

2. Stir the sugar and vanilla extract into the filling.

3. Beat the egg to a froth. Slowly drizzle the egg into the filling, stirring as you go. Stop when the filling is well moistened, and discard the remainder of the egg.

4. Prepare the dough as directed in the Old-Fashioned Coffeecake Wreath recipe up to and including Step 7. Spread the poppy seed filling over the dough, and complete the wreath by following Steps 9 through 15.

PASTRIES

ÉCLAIRS

ÉCLAIR PUFFS

I cup water

¹/₂ cup (I stick) butter

I cup all purpose
flour

¹/₄ teaspoon salt

4 eggs

**CUSTARD
FILLING**

3 cups milk

²/₃ cup sugar

3 tablespoons
cornstarch

¹/₂ teaspoon salt

4 egg yolks

I teaspoon vanilla
extract

*Many good cooks are intimidated by puff pastry, which forms the
containers for the cream or the custard in cream puffs and éclairs.
This recipe will show you how very easy it is to make delicious
chocolate-topped éclairs. On page 150, you'll find directions
for using the same dough to create light-as-air cream puffs.*

1. To make the puffs, place the water and butter in a large saucepan, and
bring to a boil over medium heat.

2. Place the flour and salt in a small bowl, and stir to mix. Stirring constantly, add the flour mixture to the boiling water mixture. Stir until
the batter comes together in a ball, and remove from the heat.

3. Add the eggs, one at a time, to the flour mixture, beating after each
addition until thoroughly combined.

4. Lightly grease a large cookie sheet, or coat lightly with cooking spray.
Place a large spoonful of batter on the sheet, creating a 3-inch oblong
shape that is mounded high in the center. Create 11 more éclairs, spacing the pastries at least 2 inches apart to allow for puffing.

5. Bake in a preheated 400°F oven for 30 minutes. Reduce the heat to
350°F, and bake for another 5 to 7 minutes, or until golden brown and
dry. To test the éclairs, remove one (not the whole sheet) from the
oven. If it holds its shape without collapsing on itself, it is done. Place
the pan on a wire rack, and allow to cool completely.

6. While the éclairs are baking, make the custard filling. Place the milk in a medium-sized saucepan and cook over low heat until small bubbles appear around the edges. Do not permit the milk to boil.

7. Sift the sugar, cornstarch, and salt together, and stir into the scalded milk, blending well.

8. Beat the egg yolks slightly, and stir into the custard. Stirring constantly, cook over very low heat, or in a double boiler, until the custard is thick enough to coat the back of the spoon. Allow to cool, and stir in the vanilla extract.

9. The traditional way to fill the éclairs is to cut a slit in the side and pipe in the prepared custard. An easier way is to cut off the tops with a serrated knife, spoon in the custard, and pop the tops back into place. I prefer this method because it gives you the opportunity to gently remove any doughy pieces from the inside.

10. To make the glaze, place the chocolate and butter in a small microwave-safe bowl, and heat on high for 15 to 20 seconds, or until melted. Alternatively, heat in a double boiler until melted. Stir until the chocolate and butter are well blended.

11. Top the éclairs with the glaze and set aside for 20 minutes, or until the glaze has hardened, before serving.

CHOCOLATE GLAZE

4 ounces German sweet chocolate

2 tablespoons butter

YIELD: **10** CROISSANTS

$^1\!/_2$ cup milk

$^1\!/_2$ tablespoon butter, softened

1 tablespoon sugar

$^1\!/_2$ teaspoon salt

$^1\!/_2$ package (1 rounded teaspoon) dry yeast

1 $^1\!/_4$ cups all purpose flour, sifted

$^1\!/_2$ cup (1 stick) butter, softened

OLD-FASHIONED CROISSANTS

*Made the old time-honored way, these croissants are
rich, flaky, and delicious, a true testament to the
pastry chef's artistry and tenacity. All good things
come to those who wait. These will test your patience.*

1. Place the milk in a small saucepan, and cook over low heat until small bubbles appear around the edges. Add the butter, sugar, and salt, and stir until the sugar is dissolved.

2. Transfer the milk mixture to a large mixing bowl, and set aside to cool. When lukewarm, stir in the yeast. Allow to sit until frothy.

3. Slowly add the flour to the milk mixture, stirring until all is incorporated. Turn the dough onto a floured board, and knead until smooth and elastic. Form into a ball.

4. Place the ball of dough in a large, clean, lightly greased bowl, turning the dough so that all sides are lightly greased. Cover and let rise in a warm place for 1$^1\!/_2$ to 2 hours, or until doubled in size.

5. Place the covered bowl of dough in the refrigerator. After about 1 hour, or when thoroughly chilled, turn the dough onto a lightly floured board and knead a few times.

6. Using a rolling pin, roll the dough into a rectangle about $^1\!/_4$ inch thick. With the long edge facing you, dot a quarter of the softened butter evenly over the dough.

7. Mentally divide the dough into thirds. Fold the right third of dough onto the middle third. Fold the left third on top. You now have a smaller rectangle comprised of three layers of dough.

8. Swing the dough around so that the long end is facing you, and roll out to a thickness of ¼ inch. Dot a quarter of the softened butter evenly over the dough.

9. Repeat Steps 7 and 8 three times.

10. Transfer the dough to a cookie sheet, cover lightly, and refrigerate until thoroughly chilled, around 2 hours.

11. Place the dough on a lightly floured board, and roll to a thickness of ¼ inch. Using a sharp knife, cut the dough into five 3½-inch squares. Then cut each square into 2 triangles.

12. Starting at the long end of a triangle, roll the dough into a log. Lightly grease a large cookie sheet, or coat lightly with cooking spray. Place each roll on the sheet, arranging it point side down so it doesn't unroll in the oven, and curve into a crescent shape. Refrigerate again for 30 minutes.

13. Bake the rolls in a preheated 350°F oven for 15 to 20 minutes, or until browned. If you have doubts about the rolls being cooked, take one out of the oven and break it open. If the dough looks damp, return the croissants to the oven for another few minutes.

VARIATION

I've enjoyed many buttery, flaky croissants with my café au lait in France, but I don't believe I've ever been offered a chocolate croissant at a sidewalk café in Paris. Perhaps this is an American invention. If you like chocolate, you'll be glad the Americans came up with the idea!

To make Chocolate Croissants, follow Steps 1 through 11 of the Old-Fashioned Croissants recipe. Before rolling the croissants into logs as outlined in Step 12, place 4 chocolate chips in the middle of the long edge and roll them into the log as you go. Continue with the recipe as directed, and serve warm while the chocolate in the pocket is still gooey. These delicate delights should make your guests take notice!

BAKLAVA

PASTRY

1 pound phyllo dough (about 24 leaves)

1 1/2 cups (3 sticks) butter

FILLING

2 cups finely chopped walnuts

1/2 cup finely chopped almonds

1/3 cup sugar

2 teaspoons ground cinnamon

1 teaspoon ground cloves

1/4 teaspoon ground cardamom

Baklava is made with buttered layers of phyllo leaves that are filled with nuts and spices, drenched in a rich honey syrup, and served as flaky diamonds. Just reading through this recipe will make you long for a sunny table overlooking the blue Aegean sea.

1. To prepare the pastry, thaw the phyllo dough as directed on the package, either overnight in the refrigerator or for 2 hours at room temperature. After you open the package, count out 8 leaves for the top layer and set aside. Cover both stacks of the delicate leaves with moistened cloths so that the dough doesn't dry out and break.

2. Clarify the butter by putting it in a small saucepan over low heat. Cook very slowly until foam rises to the top. Skim off and discard the foam. Then carefully ladle the clarified butter into a small bowl and set aside. Discard the milky remains.

3. To prepare the filling, place all of the filling ingredients in a medium-sized bowl, and stir to mix. Set aside.

4. Butter a 10-x-13-inch baking pan. Lay 1 sheet of phyllo on the bottom of the pan, and brush it with clarified butter. Repeat until you have built up a total of 8 layers of buttered phyllo. This is the bottom foundation of the pastry.

5. Sprinkle a fourth of the filling mixture over the pastry.

6. Lay 1 sheet of phyllo over the filling, and brush with clarified butter. Repeat twice, for a total of 3 layers of buttered sheets over the filling. Sprinkle a fourth of the filling mixture over the pastry.

7. Repeat Step 6 two more times, or until all except the 8 reserved sheets of dough have been used.

8. To assemble the top layer, lay a sheet of phyllo over the last layer of filling, and brush with clarified butter. Repeat until all 8 sheets have been used, buttering each layer. Brush with butter.

9. Using a sharp serrated knife, cut the layers of phyllo into diamond shapes about 1 inch wide by 2 inches long. Be very sure to cut through all layers, as this will insure that the syrup, which goes on after baking, will be able to travel throughout the pastry.

10. Bake in a preheated 350°F oven for 60 to 90 minutes, or until the baklava has puffed a bit and turned a rich golden hue.

11. While the pastry is baking, make the syrup by combining the water, sugar, cloves, and cinnamon in a medium-sized saucepan. Cook over medium heat, stirring to dissolve the sugar. When the syrup bubbles, reduce the heat and allow it to simmer for 15 to 20 minutes, or until somewhat reduced and thickened.

12. Remove the syrup from the heat, and remove and discard the cloves and cinnamon stick. Blend in the honey and, if desired, stir in the rum. Set aside. The syrup should be warm, not hot, when poured over the pastry.

13. When the pastry comes out of the oven, pour on the warm syrup as evenly as possible. Cover the pan with aluminum foil, and allow the baklava to rest overnight at room temperature so that the syrup will permeate every layer. Stored in a covered container, baklava will keep nicely for up to a month. Honey is one of Mother Nature's oldest and most effective preservatives.

SYRUP

2 cups water

1 cup sugar

4 whole cloves

1 cinnamon stick, broken

1 cup honey

$\frac{1}{2}$ cup dark rum (optional)

CREAM PUFFS

YIELD: **12** CREAM PUFFS

I recipe Éclairs
(page 144) minus
custard filling

**WHIPPED CREAM
FILLING**

2 cups heavy cream

4–6 tablespoons
powdered sugar

½ teaspoon vanilla
extract

*A cream puff is much like an éclair. But instead of the custard filling,
these puffs enclose easy-to-make whipped cream.
Nothing could be more elegant!*

1. Prepare the batter as directed in Steps 1 through 3 of the Éclairs recipe.

2. Lightly grease a large cookie sheet, or coat lightly with cooking spray. Place a large spoonful of batter on the sheet, creating a 2-inch round and mounding the batter high in the center. Create 11 more puffs, spacing the pastries at least 2 inches apart to allow for spreading.

3. Bake in a preheated 400°F oven for 30 minutes. Reduce the heat to 350°F, and bake for another 5 to 7 minutes, or until golden brown and dry. To test the cream puffs, remove one (not the whole sheet) from the oven. If it holds its shape without collapsing on itself, it is done. Place the pan on a wire rack, and allow to cool completely.

4. While the cream puffs are cooling, prepare the whipped cream filling. Place the heavy cream in a medium-sized bowl, and use an electric mixer to whip until very soft peaks form. Add the powdered sugar, using the larger amount if you like a sweeter filling. Add the vanilla, and continue whipping until the cream is very stiff and holds its shape.

5. Fill and glaze the cream puffs as directed in Steps 9 through 11 of the Éclairs recipe, and serve.

SCONES, BUNS, AND BREADS

AEBLESKIVERS

YIELD: 12–15
AEBLESKIVERS

You need a special pan to make aebleskivers—the unique Danish delights that are somewhat like doughnuts. The pan has seven half-moon depressions that are slightly larger than golf balls. The trick is to start the batter sizzling over medium heat, and then turn the balls of batter round and round quickly with a fork. If you'd love to try making aebleskivers and need a pan, check the Resource List on page 184.

1. Separate the egg, dropping the yolk into a large mixing bowl and the white into a small mixing bowl.

2. Using an electric mixer, beat the egg white until stiff peaks form. Set aside.

3. Add the buttermilk and butter to the egg yolk, and beat together.

4. Sift the flour, sugar, baking powder, baking soda, and salt together. Add the flour mixture to the liquid mixture, beating with an electric mixer or by hand until smooth. Fold in the egg white.

5. Preheat the aebleskiver pan over medium heat. When hot, place 1 scant tablespoon of canola oil in the bottom of each aebleskiver pan cup. Give the oil a few seconds to get hot.

6. Pour about 2 tablespoons of batter into each cup. Watch closely. As soon as the batter begins to puff and bubble around the edges, roll it around with a fork. Continue cooking, turning the ball to keep it from burning, until the batter is fully cooked all the way around.

7. Serve hot with a dollop of jam and a sprinkling of powdered sugar.

1 egg

1 cup buttermilk

2 tablespoons butter, melted

1 cup all purpose flour

1 tablespoon sugar

1 teaspoon baking powder

1/4 teaspoon baking soda

1/4 teaspoon salt

Canola oil for frying

MYRTLE'S OLD-FASHIONED FRIED CAKES

YIELD: 12–18
DOUGHNUTS

1 egg

1/2 cup sugar

1/2 cup milk

3 tablespoons butter,
melted

2 cups all purpose
flour

2 teaspoons baking
powder

1/4 teaspoon salt

1/8 teaspoon ground
nutmeg

Vegetable oil for frying,
preferably canola

1/2 cup powdered sugar
(optional)

*When I was growing up, we had a cook named Myrtle who made the
best doughnuts ever. My sister and I stood at her elbow and pestered
her until she finally sighed with irritation and gave us a bowlful
of "undressed" doughnut holes. They were so good, it was hard
to wait for them to cool. Although I don't have Myrtle's recipe,
these delicious "cakes" come very close, and are meant
to be paired with a steaming cup of coffee.*

1. Place the egg in a medium-sized mixing bowl, and beat with an electric mixer until frothy. Continue beating while slowly adding the
sugar.

2. Place the milk in a small bowl, and stir in the melted butter. Gradually
add the milk mixture to the egg mixture, beating continually.

3. Sift the flour, baking powder, salt, and nutmeg together, and beat the
flour mixture into the batter a third at a time. Cover the bowl, and
refrigerate for an hour or longer. This will make the soft, sticky dough
easier to work with.

4. Turn the dough onto a well-floured board. Knead several times,
adding additional flour as needed. With a floured rolling pin, roll the
dough to about 1/4-inch thickness.

5. Using a floured doughnut cutter, cut the dough into 12 to 18 doughnuts. (If you don't have a doughnut cutter, use a thin-rimmed 2 1/2-
inch glass to cut the outer circle, and the top of a small bottle to cut
out the center.) Air-dry the dough for 20 minutes. This will prevent
the doughnuts from absorbing too much oil while frying.

6. Place at least 2 inches of oil in a large soup pot and, using a cooking thermometer, heat the oil to 370°F. If you don't have a thermometer, test the temperature of the oil by dropping in a cube of stale bread. The bread should brown—but not burn—in less than a minute, about 50 seconds.

7. Using a spatula, ease the doughnuts into the hot oil one at a time. Don't overcrowd the pan or the temperature of the oil will drop, and the doughnuts will absorb fat and get very greasy. You may drop in the holes at the same time. Brown the doughnuts on one side, then turn and brown on the second side. The doughnuts should take 2 to 3 minutes in total, but the holes will cook much more quickly.

8. Lift the doughnuts and holes out of the pan with a slotted spoon, and transfer them to a pan or plate covered with a double thickness of paper towels. If the temperature of the oil has been kept constant, the paper will hardly be marked with oil, and the doughnuts will be crisp and light.

9. Sift the powdered sugar over the doughnuts if desired, and serve warm.

YIELD: 10–12 BUNS

UPSIDE-DOWN STICKY BUNS

DOUGH

$^1/_2$ cup lukewarm water

1 package ($^1/_2$ ounce) dry yeast

2$^1/_4$ cups all purpose flour, divided

$^1/_2$ cup butter, softened

$^1/_4$ cup sugar

1 egg

$^1/_2$ teaspoon salt

FILLING

$^1/_4$ cup butter, softened

$^1/_4$ cup dark brown sugar

$^1/_2$ cup broken pecan pieces

There's no more enticing smell wafting from the kitchen than yeast dough a'rising. These are the good old-fashioned kind of sticky buns that are impossible to resist. They take awhile to prepare, but they're worth the wait.

1. To make the dough, place the lukewarm water in a small mixing bowl, and stir in the yeast. When frothy, stir in $^1/_2$ cup of the flour. Cover and let rise until a light sponge forms, 30 to 45 minutes.

2. Place the butter in a large mixing bowl, and cream with an electric mixer until light. Beat the sugar into the butter. When well incorporated, beat in the egg and salt. Add the yeast mixture, and beat until blended.

3. Gradually add the remaining flour to the dough, beating after each addition. When the dough becomes too stiff to work with the mixer, use a dough hook or incorporate the rest of the flour by hand.

4. Turn the dough onto a floured board and knead until smooth and elastic. Place the dough in a clean, lightly greased bowl, cover, and let rise for 1$^1/_2$ to 2 hours, or until doubled in size.

5. Punch down the dough, and transfer to a floured board. Using a rolling pin, roll into a rectangle of $^1/_4$- to $^1/_2$-inch thickness.

6. To fill the dough, first spread it with the softened butter. Then sprinkle evenly with the brown sugar and pecan pieces.

7. Starting at one of the long sides, roll the dough into a log, pressing lightly as you roll to encourage the pecan pieces to stay in place. With a sharp knife, cut the log into 1-inch slices.

8. To dress the cake pan, melt the butter in an 8- or 9-inch round metal (not glass) pan, and swirl to coat the bottom. Sprinkle with the brown sugar and pecan pieces.

9. Lay the slices flat in the dressed pan. Cover and let rise for 30 to 45 minutes, or until the buns have doubled in size.

10. Bake in a preheated 350°F oven for 20 to 30 minutes, or until lightly browned. Allow to cool for a few minutes. Then, using potholders, put a plate over the pan and flip upside down. Tap the bottom of the pan to encourage the buns to slide out, but leave the pan in place for a minute or 2 so that all the lovely sticky syrup runs out and covers the buns. Serve warm.

DRESSING FOR PAN

¼ cup butter

¼ cup dark brown sugar

½ cup broken pecan pieces

YIELD: 10–12 BUNS

DOUGH

1/2 cup milk, divided

1/2 cup water, divided

1/2 cup sugar, divided

2 packages (1/2 ounce each) dry yeast

4 1/2 cups all purpose flour, divided

1/2 cup butter, softened

1/2 teaspoon salt

2 eggs

I teaspoon vanilla extract

TOPPING

I cup all purpose flour

I cup powdered sugar

6 tablespoons cold butter, cut into pieces

2 1/2 tablespoons cocoa powder

1 1/2 tablespoons ground cinnamon

CONCHAS

A friend tells me that pan dulce (sweet bread) is traditionally served with the breakfast coffee in Mexico, and that the best-loved pan dulce is decorated with sugary little conchas—shells. This Americanized version uses a sweet egg-enriched yeast dough, but the traditional concha topping remains the same. Prepare it for a taste of Mexico.

1. To make the dough, combine 1/4 cup of the milk and 1/4 cup of the water in a small saucepan, and heat to lukewarm. Remove the pan from the heat, add 1 1/2 teaspoons of the sugar, and stir until dissolved. Stir in the yeast, and let sit until frothy.

2. Place 1/2 cup of the flour in a small mixing bowl. Make a well in the center, pour in the milk mixture, and stir until thoroughly combined. Cover and set aside to rise for 20 minutes.

3. Place the butter in a large mixing bowl, and cream with an electric mixer until light. Beating continually, gradually add the remaining sugar and the salt until very creamy.

4. Place the eggs and vanilla extract in a small bowl, and beat to a froth. Add gradually to the butter mixture, beating until thoroughly blended.

5. Sift the remaining 4 cups of flour. Gradually beat about half of the flour into the butter mixture, alternating it with the remaining 1/4 cup of milk and 1/4 cup of water, until well blended. Then beat in the yeast mixture.

6. Add the remaining flour gradually to the dough. When too stiff to work, use a dough hook or turn the dough onto a floured board and knead in the remaining flour with your hands.

7. Place the dough in a clean, lightly greased bowl. Cover and let rise for $1\frac{1}{2}$ to 2 hours, or until doubled in size.

8. When you're ready to continue, prepare the topping by sifting the flour and powdered sugar into a small mixing bowl. Transfer about $\frac{1}{2}$ cup of the mixture to your food processor, add the cold butter, and whirl until the mixture resembles very fine bread crumbs. Alternatively, place the mixture in a small bowl and cut in the butter with 2 knives or a pastry cutter. Return the mixture to the bowl, and blend thoroughly with a fork.

9. Transfer half of the topping mixture to another bowl. Stir the cocoa into one half and the cinnamon into the other, mixing each until thoroughly blended. Cover the bowls and set aside until you have formed the buns.

10. Remove the dough from the refrigerator, and turn it onto a lightly floured board. Divide the dough equally into 10 to 12 pieces, and roll each piece of dough into a ball.

11. Lightly grease a large cookie sheet or coat lightly with cooking spray. Arrange the buns on the sheet, spacing them about 2 inches apart. If you need more room, prepare another sheet.

12. To top the buns, lightly flour your hands and form 1-inch diameter balls of the topping mixtures, making half the balls with the cocoa topping and half with the cinnamon topping. Using the palms of your hands, firmly flatten each ball into a circle.

13. Place one circle on top of each bun, pressing down firmly. If you have a Mexican shell-shaped decorative cutter or similar cookie cutter, now's the time to use it. If not, use the tip of a sharp knife to scallop the top edge like that of a shell and draw in the grooves.

14. Allow the buns to rise, uncovered, for 2½ to 3 hours, or until puffed, but not doubled.

15. Bake in a preheated 375°F oven for 10 to 12 minutes, or until the conchas are lightly browned around the edges and springy to the touch. Place the pan on a wire rack and allow to cool completely before serving.

YIELD: **8–10** ROUNDS

5 cups all purpose flour, divided

1 package (½ ounce) dry yeast

½ teaspoon sugar

1 teaspoon salt

½ teaspoon baking powder

2 cups hot water

Vegetable oil for frying, preferably canola

Powdered sugar (optional)

INDIAN FRY BREAD

I lived in Arizona for close to fifteen years, and during that time,
I was introduced to Indian fry bread and came to love it.
I'm not sure this is an original dish of the Native Americans of old,
but it sure is good. A bonus is that Indian fry bread stands
in beautifully for pita bread. In fact, I like it better.
Fold in half while warm, fill as desired, and enjoy the crunch.

1. Place 3 cups of the flour in a large bowl. Stir in the yeast, sugar, salt, and baking powder, mixing well. While beating with an electric mixer, add the hot water slowly until thoroughly mixed.

2. Slowly add the remainder of the flour, working it in by hand as needed. The dough should be soft, but not sticky.

3. Turn the dough onto a lightly floured board, and knead until smooth and elastic, adding a very little flour as needed to keep the dough from sticking.

4. Shape the dough into a ball, and place it in a clean, lightly greased bowl. Cover and let rise for about an hour, or until doubled in size.

5. Punch the dough down. Dust your fingers with flour, and break off (don't cut) enough dough to form a ball 2 to 3 inches in diameter. With the palm of your hand, flatten the dough into a circle about 1/4 inch thick. Make a 1-inch cut through the center of the circle with a sharp knife.

6. Tear off a large sheet of foil, and arrange the circles on the foil as you make them. When all are completed, cover lightly and let rest for 30 minutes.

7. Place 2 inches of oil in a large soup pot and, using a cooking thermometer, preheat the oil to 365°F. If you don't have a thermometer, test the temperature of the oil by dropping in a cube of stale bread. The bread should brown—but not burn—in about 2 minutes.

8. Using a spatula, slide 1 circle of dough into the hot oil. When the underside is golden brown, turn and cook the other side. It will take 3 to 5 minutes to cook each circle.

9. Lift the fry bread out of the pan with a slotted spoon, and transfer it to a pan or plate covered with a double thickness of paper towels.

10. Sift some powdered sugar over the bread, if desired, and serve warm.

YIELD: 1 LOAF	# HEALTHY FRUITY BREAKFAST BREAD

FRUITS

¹/₄ cup dried apricots

¹/₄ cup pitted, quartered dates

¹/₄ cup dark or golden raisins

¹/₄ cup coarsely chopped walnuts

¹/₄ cup sunflower seeds (optional)

1 tablespoon flour

BATTER

1 egg

¹/₂ cup sour cream

¹/₄ cup honey

1 tablespoon canola oil

1 cup whole wheat flour

¹/₂ teaspoon baking soda

Although I call this fruit-and-nut-filled treat a breakfast bread, you'll also enjoy it as an afternoon snack or a healthy dessert— accompanied, of course, by a steaming cup of coffee.

1. Place the apricots in a small heatproof bowl, and cover with hot water. Set aside for 10 minutes.

2. Drain the apricots, pat dry with a paper towel, and cut into pieces.

3. Place the apricots in a medium-sized bowl with the dates, raisins, walnuts, and sunflower seeds, if desired, and toss to mix. Dust with the tablespoon of flour, tossing to coat, and set aside.

4. To make the batter, place the egg in a large mixing bowl, and beat to a froth with an electric mixer. Beat in the sour cream, honey, and canola oil.

5. Sift the flour and baking soda together. Gradually add the flour mixture to the egg mixture, beating until smooth. Stir in the fruit mixture just until blended.

6. Lightly grease a 7-x-4-inch loaf pan, or lightly coat with cooking spray. Pour the batter into the pan.

7. Place the pan in a cold oven, and set the oven at 350°F. (Do *not* preheat the oven.) Resist the urge to peek until 30 minutes have passed. The bread is done when a toothpick inserted in the center comes out clean. If not, return the bread to the oven for another 5 to 10 minutes.

8. Cool the pan on a wire rack for 5 minutes, then turn the bread out. Return the loaf to the rack, and allow to cool completely. Cut into thick slices and serve.

SOPAIPILLAS

YIELD: 10–12
SOPAIPILLAS

I cup all purpose flour

I teaspoon baking powder

$\frac{1}{2}$ teaspoon salt

I tablespoon butter, softened

$\frac{1}{3}$ cup cold water

Vegetable oil for frying, preferably canola

Honey for drizzling

*My grandson, age six, personally orders sopaipillas (so-pah-pee-ahs)
for dessert when we go to our favorite Mexican restaurant.
We are all happy to join him. These deep-fried morsels are
dipped in honey or drizzled with honey at the table. Note that
they are similar to Indian Fry Bread, which is found on page 158.*

1. Sift the flour, baking powder, and salt into a large mixing bowl. Rub in the butter or cut it in with 2 knives until the mixture resembles a coarse meal. Sprinkle in the cold water a little at a time, using just enough to make a stiff dough that will hold together.

2. Turn the dough onto a lightly floured board, and knead until smooth and elastic. This is not a yeast dough, so it won't "push back" as much as a yeast dough does. Cover the dough and let it rest for 10 minutes.

3. With a floured rolling pin, roll the dough to about $\frac{1}{8}$-inch thickness. Using a sharp knife, cut into $2\frac{1}{2}$-inch squares.

4. Place at least 2 inches of oil in a large soup pot and, using a cooking thermometer, heat the oil to 370°F. If you don't have a thermometer, test the temperature of the oil by dropping in a cube of stale bread. The bread should brown—but not burn—in about 50 seconds.

5. Using a spatula, slide 2 or 3 squares of dough into the hot oil. Cook, turning with a slotted spoon, until the sopaipillas puff up nicely and are evenly brown.

6. Lift the sopaipillas out of the pan with a slotted spoon, and transfer them to a pan or plate covered with a double thickness of paper towels. Serve hot with honey on the side for drizzling or dipping.

1 ½ cups self-rising flour, divided

2 tablespoons cold butter, cut into small chunks

½ cup grated Cheddar cheese

½ teaspoon dry mustard

¼ teaspoon salt

1 egg

Milk

SAVORY CHEESE SCONES

If you've been put off by those hard, dry things that Americans have come to accept as scones, please try this recipe. These tender, flavorful scones rise proudly in the oven, becoming temptingly light and high.

1. Place ½ cup of the flour in a food processor. Add the butter, and process until the mixture looks like fine breadcrumbs. Alternatively, place the flour in a medium-sized bowl and cut in the butter with 2 knives or a pastry cutter until the proper consistency is reached.

2. If the flour and butter were combined in a food processor, transfer the flour mixture to a medium-sized mixing bowl. Add the remainder of the flour and the cheese, dry mustard, and salt, and blend with a fork until well combined.

3. Place the egg in a measuring cup and whip with a fork until frothy. Add just enough milk to the beaten egg to measure ⅔ cup. Reserve 1½ tablespoons of the mixture for glazing the top of the scones.

4. Make a well in the dry ingredients, and add all of the egg mixture, except for the reserved portion, stirring with a fork to make a soft dough. If you have dry spots, drizzle in a little more milk.

5. Turn the dough onto a lightly floured board and knead a few times. Pat or roll out the dough to a thickness of about ¾ inch. Using a cookie cutter or floured glass, cut the dough into 2-inch rounds.

6. Lightly grease a large cookie sheet or coat lightly with cooking spray, and arrange the dough rounds on the sheet, spacing them about 2 inches apart. Brush the tops of the scones with the reserved egg mixture.

7. Bake in a preheated 425°F oven for about 18 minutes, or until the scones are lightly browned. To test, fork open a scone to see if the interior is fully cooked. If not, return to the oven for another 2 minutes.

8. Serve warm from the oven, split, and lightly buttered.

SWEET CURRANT SCONES

*These scones are slightly sweet, high and light, rich and crumbly—
as good as any I've ever had.*

1. To make the dough, place ½ cup of the flour in a food processor. Add the butter, and process until the mixture looks like fine breadcrumbs. Alternatively, place the flour in a medium-sized bowl and cut in the butter with 2 knives or a pastry cutter until the proper consistency is reached.

2. If the flour and butter were combined in a food processor, transfer the flour mixture to a medium-sized mixing bowl. Sift the remaining flour together with the sugar, baking powder, and salt, and add to the bowl, along with the currants. Mix with a fork to combine well.

3. Add the milk to the bowl, stirring quickly with a fork to make a soft dough. If you have any dry spots, drizzle in a little more milk.

4. Turn the dough onto a lightly floured board, and knead a few times. Pat or roll out the dough to the thickness of about ¾ inch. Using a cookie cutter or floured glass, cut the dough into 2-inch rounds.

5. Lightly grease a large cookie sheet or coat lightly with cooking spray, and arrange the dough rounds on the sheet, spacing them about 2 inches apart.

YIELD: 6–8 SCONES

DOUGH

2 cups all purpose flour, divided

3 tablespoons cold butter, cut into small chunks

2 tablespoons sugar

2 teaspoons baking powder

½ teaspoon salt

¼ cup dried currants

¾ cup milk

GLAZE

1 egg

1 tablespoon milk

Sugar

6. To make the glaze, place the egg and milk in a small bowl, and beat to a froth. Brush the tops of the scones with a little of the mixture and sprinkle with the sugar.

7. Bake in a preheated 425°F oven for about 10 minutes, or until the scones are lightly browned. To test, fork open a scone to see if the interior is fully cooked. If not, return to the oven for another 2 minutes.

8. Serve warm from the oven, split, and dressed with a little butter and your best jam. I favor black raspberry. Or, for a truly traditional presentation, serve with jam and clotted cream, which is available in the dairy section of some supermarkets and specialty stores.

PUDDINGS AND CUSTARDS

COFFEE ZABAGLIONE

YIELD: **4** SERVINGS

¹/₄ cup hot water

2 teaspoons instant coffee granules

6 egg yolks

2 tablespoons honey

In Italy, this rich custard is made with Marsala,
an Italian dessert wine. This version is laced, instead,
with coffee, creating a luscious dessert that can be paired
with plain coffee or with your favorite coffee specialty drink.

1. Place water in the bottom of a double boiler, and bring to a simmer over medium-high heat. If you don't have a double boiler, select a pan that will rest over (not in) a larger pan that will hold the water.

2. Place the hot water and coffee granules in a small dish, and stir until the coffee is dissolved. Set aside.

3. Take the top of the double boiler off the heat, place the egg yolks in the pan, and beat with an electric mixer until very light. Add the honey and beat for an additional 60 seconds, or until combined.

4. Place the top of the double boiler over the simmering water, and very slowly drizzle in the coffee mixture while beating with an electric mixer. Continue beating for 2 to 3 minutes, or until the custard becomes very thick and very creamy. Just when you think the custard will never thicken, it will. Transfer the mixture to a bowl, cover, and refrigerate until chilled.

5. To serve, spoon the zabaglione into four demitasse cups. These are small servings, but zabaglione is so rich that even this little bit is very satisfying. Expect applause.

COFFEE-CUSTARD FLAN

CARAMEL LAYER

¾ cup sugar

COFFEE CUSTARD

3 cups whole milk

⅓ cup sugar

⅛ teaspoon salt

1½ tablespoons instant coffee granules

½ teaspoon vanilla extract

1 whole egg

2 egg yolks

Flan was originally a Spanish specialty, but long ago,
this rich custard made its way into the mainstream.
Traditionally, it is prepared in a flanera—
a special pan that is sized to go into its own water bath.
But you can improvise, as I do, and still enjoy delicious results.

1. To make the caramel layer, place the sugar in a small, heavy skillet, and cook over very low heat until the sugar begins to break down. Shake the pan, but resist the temptation to stir. When the sugar is dissolved, increase the heat and stir, preferably with a wooden spoon, until the sugar bubbles and browns.

2. Quickly pour the caramelized sugar into an 8-inch flan pan or cake pan, and swirl until the liquid rolls up the sides and coats the bottom. Work carefully. The caramel is very hot and will burn if you're careless. Set aside while you prepare the custard.

3. Combine the milk, sugar, and salt in a large, heavy saucepan, and cook over low heat, stirring, until the sugar has dissolved. Bring slowly to a boil, stirring occasionally. When bubbling, stir in the coffee granules. Remove the saucepan from the heat, stir in the vanilla, and allow to cool.

4. Place the whole egg and 2 yolks in a small bowl, and beat together until frothy. When the milk and coffee mixture has cooled to lukewarm, stir the eggs into the milk. Pour the mixture through a strainer into the caramel-coated pan.

5. Place the flan pan in a second pan filled with enough hot water to come a third of the way to halfway up the sides of the flan pan. Bake in a preheated 325°F for 45 to 60 minutes, or until a toothpick inserted in the center of the custard comes out clean.

6. Remove the pan carefully from the oven, and allow the flan to sit in the water bath for 15 minutes to set the custard. Transfer the flan pan to a wire rack and cool completely before refrigerating. Refrigerate for at least 4 hours before serving.

7. To unmold, run a knife blade around the edges of the flan, and place the pan in a pan of hot water for a few minutes. This caramel is slightly syrupy, so turn the flan onto a serving platter with a rim. Drizzle any caramel that remains in the pan around the edges, and cut into wedges to serve, refrigerating any leftovers.

CAFÉ ET CRÈME BRULÉE

YIELD: 4–6 SERVINGS

COFFEE CUSTARD

¼ cup cold water

1 envelope (.25 ounce) unflavored gelatin

1 teaspoon hot water

2 teaspoons instant coffee granules*

4 egg yolks

⅓ cup sugar

2 cups heavy cream

SUGAR TOPPING

⅛ cup brown sugar

⅛ cup sugar

* If you like caffè latte, 2 teaspoons of instant coffee will perfectly flavor this custard. If you are an espresso lover and want a more intense flavor, use 3 to 4 teaspoons of instant coffee dissolved in 1½ to 2 teaspoons of hot water.

I make Café et Crème Brulée often because it's a favorite of one of my darling daughters-in-law. This recipe calls for gelatin and is not baked, so it's not the classic brulée, but it's awfully good. You might be interested to know that the word brulée comes from bruler, which means "to burn." It refers, of course, to the burned (caramelized) sugar crust that crowns the custard cream. Professional chefs caramelize the sugar with a small blow torch. The rest of us have to use a broiler.

1. To make the custard, place the cold water in a small cup. Sprinkle with the gelatin and set aside.

2. Place the hot water and instant coffee in another small cup, and stir to dissolve. Set aside.

3. Place the egg yolks in a small mixing bowl, and beat with an electric mixer or whisk until thick. Beat in the sugar and dissolved coffee.

4. Place 1 cup of the cream in a medium-sized heavy saucepan. Add the egg mixture and stir until smoothly combined.

5. Cook the custard over very low heat, stirring continually, for 5 to 7 minutes, or until the mixture thickens and coats the back of a spoon. Success or failure comes from this step. It's necessary to cook the eggs, but if you allow the custard to boil, it will curdle.

6. Remove the saucepan from the heat and add the softened gelatin, stirring until fully dissolved. When well combined, stir in the remaining cup of cream.

7. Pour the custard into 4 to 6 lightly buttered heatproof custard cups or an 8-inch heatproof baking pan or pie pan. Refrigerate for 2 hours, or until very cold.

8. When the custard is thoroughly chilled, make the topping by combining the sugars, and sprinkle the mixture evenly over the top of the custards. Smooth with the back of a spoon.

9. Place the custards under a preheated broiler, as close to the heat source as possible, for 3 to 5 minutes, or until the sugar bubbles. The idea is to caramelize the sugar before the custard melts.

10. Return the custards to the refrigerator and chill thoroughly before serving, about 1 hour.

Special Sauces

You don't have to spend hours baking a cake or a plate of biscotti to enjoy a special dessert. These rich coffee-laced sauces take just minutes to make, and can transform a wedge of store-bought angel food cake or a scoop of vanilla ice cream into a gourmet treat. To make the sauces suitable for large gatherings or late-night binges, use decaf coffee, and even the youngest members of your family will be able to enjoy these delights.

NUTTY COFFEE SAUCE

Because I am nuts for nuts, this sauce is a personal favorite. However, there's nothing worse than soggy nuts. To make sure they stay crisp and crunchy, add the nuts to the sauce just before serving or sprinkle them over the top. Use your favorite nuts—pecans and walnuts are both good choices— and spoon over vanilla ice cream.

YIELD: ABOUT 2 CUPS

I cup light brown sugar, packed

I tablespoon cornstarch

I cup strong coffee

$1/4$ cup light corn syrup

$1/4$ cup butter

$1/2$ cup chopped nuts

1. Place the brown sugar and cornstarch in a medium-sized saucepan, and stir to combine. Stir in the coffee and corn syrup, blending well.

2. Place the saucepan over medium-high heat and, stirring occasionally, bring to a boil. Allow the sauce to boil for 2 minutes, still stirring occasionally. Skim off any foam.

3. Remove the saucepan from the heat, and stir in the butter. Allow to cool for about 10 minutes.

4. Serve the sauce warm or cold, adding the nuts just before serving or sprinkling them over the top.

ADULTS-ONLY MOCHA SAUCE

This marvelous sauce calls for two liqueurs, explaining why it's for adults only.

YIELD: ABOUT 1 CUP

$^1/_2$ cup brown sugar, firmly packed

$^1/_4$ cup cocoa powder

4 teaspoons cornstarch

I teaspoon instant coffee granules

$^1/_2$ cup water

2 tablespoons light corn syrup

I teaspoon crème de cacao

I teaspoon coffee liqueur

$^1/_2$ teaspoon vanilla extract

1. Place the brown sugar, cocoa powder, cornstarch, and coffee granules in a small saucepan, and stir to mix. Gradually add the water, stirring until smooth. Stir in the corn syrup.

2. Place the saucepan over medium heat and cook, stirring constantly, until the sauce bubbles and thickens slightly.

3. Remove the pot from the heat and allow to cool for 5 minutes. Stir in the liqueurs and the vanilla extract.

4. Serve the sauce warm, stirring just before using. Refrigerate any leftovers.

MOCHA SAUCE

The marriage of coffee and chocolate makes this sauce unbelievably luscious.

YIELD: ABOUT 1$^1/_2$ CUPS

$^1/_4$ cup hot water

I tablespoon instant coffee granules

$^1/_4$ cup half-and-half or heavy cream

I cup semisweet chocolate chips

I tablespoon light corn syrup

1. Place the hot water and coffee granules in a small saucepan, and stir to dissolve the coffee.

2. Place the saucepan over low heat, and whisk in the half-and-half. Bring the mixture to a boil, stirring constantly.

3. Remove the pot from the heat, and add the chocolate chips and corn syrup. Whisk until the chocolate is melted and the sauce is slightly thickened, about 5 minutes. Allow to cool slightly and serve, refrigerating any leftovers.

RICH COFFEE TIRAMISU

YIELD: 8–10 SERVINGS

24 ounces mascarpone cheese

1 cup powdered sugar

1 cup rum, divided

1 cup heavy cream

2 large eggs

1¾ cups granulated sugar, divided

4 cups very strong coffee

18 ladyfingers

Semisweet chocolate curls or cocoa powder (optional)

When we were in Italy a few years ago, we had the great good fortune to stay with friends in Latina, a small "bedroom" community that serves Rome commuters. One memorable evening, we enjoyed a delicious pasta dish, capped by a rich and creamy homemade tiramisu dessert. What a feast! Enjoy this tiramisu with tiny cups of espresso and you'll feel as if you, too, are in a charming Italian village.

1. Place the cheese, powdered sugar, and ½ cup of the rum in a large mixing bowl, and beat on low speed with an electric mixer until smooth and creamy. Add the cream, and beat on high speed until soft peaks form.

2. Place the eggs and ¼ cup of the granulated sugar in a small bowl, and beat until thick and pale. Fold the egg mixture into the cheese mixture, and set aside.

3. Place the coffee, the remaining ½ cup of rum, and the remaining 1½ cups of sugar in a small bowl, and whisk together until the sugar is dissolved.

4. One at a time, dip the ladyfingers into the coffee mixture, and arrange in a single layer over the bottom of a 2-quart glass serving bowl. Top with a third of the cheese mixture. Continue forming layers until you have 3 layers of coffee-dipped ladyfingers topped with the cheese mixture. Cover with plastic wrap and refrigerate for at least 2 hours.

5. Top the tiramisu with shaved chocolate curls or a dusting of sifted cocoa powder, if desired, and serve.

BISCOTTI

CHOCOLATE-COFFEE BISCOTTI

Chocolate and coffee are a classic combination.
Each and every bite of these crunchy cookies is a delight.

1. Place the butter and sugar in a large mixing bowl, and cream together with an electric mixer.

2. Add the unbeaten egg whites to the butter mixture, and continue beating until well combined. Scrape down the sides of the bowl as necessary.

3. Sift the flour, cocoa powder, coffee granules, and baking powder together, and gradually add to the butter mixture, beating until blended.

4. At this point, check the consistency of the dough. If it is too stiff to form with your hands, add a very little water or milk.

5. Lightly grease a large cookie sheet or coat lightly with cooking spray. Flour your hands lightly, remove the dough from the bowl, and pat it into a ball. Place the ball on the prepared sheet and form it into a flat loaf about 2 inches wide and 1 inch thick.

6. Bake in a preheated 350° oven for 15 to 18 minutes, or until the loaf develops a light crust and feels firm to the touch. To test, cut across the center of the loaf. It should cut cleanly. If still doughy, return to the oven for another few minutes.

YIELD: 12–18 COOKIES

DOUGH

$1/4$ cup butter, softened

$1/2$ cup sugar

4 egg whites

2 cups all purpose flour

$1/3$ cup cocoa powder

2 teaspoons instant coffee granules

2 teaspoons baking powder

COFFEE SUGAR ICING

$1/2$ cup powdered sugar

$1/8$ teaspoon instant coffee granules

1 tablespoon hot water

7. Place the pan on a wire rack for 5 minutes to set. Then transfer the loaf to a cutting board and use a sharp knife to cut across the loaf into $\frac{1}{2}$-inch-thick slices. Resist the temptation to make the slices thicker.

8. Arrange the cookies on the greased baking sheet in a single layer, cut side down. Use a second greased sheet, if needed.

9. Return the biscotti to the oven and continue baking until the cookies are dry and the insides are fully cooked, about another 10 minutes. Cool completely on a wire rack.

10. While the biscotti are cooling, make the icing by sifting the powdered sugar into a small mixing bowl. Dissolve the coffee granules in the hot water, and stir into the powdered sugar until smooth.

11. To eliminate the raw taste of the uncooked powdered sugar, place the icing in a microwave oven and heat on high for 20 seconds. Alternatively, place the mixture in a small saucepan and cook over low heat, stirring constantly, for 1 minute. Allow the icing to cool before using.

12. Spread a thin layer of the icing on each cookie, and allow to set before serving. Store any leftovers in an airtight tin.

ALMOND BISCOTTI

YIELD: 12–18 COOKIES

There's nothing more Italian than munching biscotti with your coffee. These homemade biscotti are crunchy, but not as hard as "store-bought." I like them better—and almond biscotti are my favorite, especially when they're topped with an almond-studded icing.

1. To make the dough, place the butter and sugar in a large mixing bowl, and cream together with an electric mixer.

2. Add the unbeaten egg whites and almond flavoring to the butter mixture, and continue beating until well combined. Scrape down the sides of the bowl as necessary.

3. Sift the flour and baking powder together and add gradually to the butter mixture, beating until blended. Blend in the almonds.

4. At this point, check the consistency of the dough. If it is too stiff to form with your hands, add a very little water or milk.

5. Lightly grease a large cookie sheet or coat lightly with cooking spray. Flour your hands lightly, remove the dough from the bowl, and pat it into a ball. Place the ball on the prepared sheet and form it into a flat loaf about 2 inches wide and 1 inch thick.

6. Bake in a preheated 350° oven for 15 to 18 minutes, or until the loaf develops a light crust and feels firm to the touch. To test, cut across the center of the loaf. It should cut cleanly. If still doughy, return to the oven for another few minutes.

7. Place the pan on a wire rack for 5 minutes to set. Then transfer the loaf to a cutting board and use a sharp knife to cut the loaf into $\frac{1}{2}$-inch-thick slices. Resist the temptation to make the slices thicker.

DOUGH

$\frac{1}{4}$ cup butter, softened

$\frac{1}{2}$ cup sugar

4 egg whites

$\frac{1}{4}$ teaspoon almond flavoring

2 $\frac{1}{3}$ cups all purpose flour

2 teaspoons baking powder

$\frac{1}{3}$ cup thinly sliced almonds

ALMOND SUGAR ICING

$\frac{1}{2}$ cup powdered sugar

1 tablespoon hot water

$\frac{1}{4}$ teaspoon almond flavoring

$\frac{1}{8}$ cup thinly sliced almonds

8. Arrange the cookies on the greased baking sheet in a single layer, cut side down. Use a second greased sheet, if needed.

9. Return the biscotti to the oven and continue baking until the cookies are dry and the insides are fully cooked, about another 10 minutes. Cool completely on a wire rack.

10. While the biscotti are cooling, make the icing by sifting the powdered sugar into a small mixing bowl. Add the hot water and flavoring, and stir well to blend thoroughly.

11. To eliminate the raw taste of the uncooked powdered sugar, place the icing in a microwave oven and heat on high for 20 seconds. Alternatively, place the mixture in a small saucepan and cook over low heat, stirring constantly, for 1 minute. Allow the icing to cool before using.

12. Spread a thin layer of the icing on each cookie, and sprinkle with the almonds while the icing is soft. Allow to set before serving. Store any leftovers in an airtight tin.

CANDY

COFFEE AND CREAM FUDGE

*If you're a coffee fanatic, you will love this fudge. Even my daughter,
who never took to coffee, is crazy over this creamy confection.
Each bite is rich and smooth, with intense coffee flavor.*

YIELD: ABOUT 1 POUND

2 cups sugar

$\frac{1}{2}$ cup brown sugar

$\frac{1}{8}$ teaspoon salt

1 $\frac{1}{4}$ cups coffee

$\frac{1}{4}$ cup heavy cream

1 tablespoon butter

1 teaspoon vanilla
extract

1. Place the sugars and salt in a medium-sized saucepan, and stir to combine. Stir in the coffee and cream.

2. Place the sugar mixture over medium heat, and cook, stirring occasionally, until it begins to simmer.

3. Turn the heat under the saucepan very low and cover. Allow to bubble for 3 minutes. Then remove the cover. This step will dissolve any sugar crystals and help insure a smooth and creamy finish.

4. Continue cooking until the mixture reaches 234°F to 238°F on a candy thermometer. Alternatively, cook to the soft-ball stage. To test, drizzle a little hot syrup into a cup of cold water. When the cooled syrup comes together when you roll it with one finger, it has reached the soft-ball stage.

5. Remove the saucepan from the heat, and add the butter and vanilla extract. Using an electric mixer, beat on high just until the syrup begins to thicken and starts to lose its shine. Quickly transfer the fudge to a buttered 8-inch pie plate or a similar pan.

6. Place the fudge in the refrigerator for about 10 minutes. Using a sharp knife, cut the fudge into squares while warm and serve.

2 cups sugar

1/2 cup cocoa powder

1/8 teaspoon salt

1 cup coffee

2 tablespoons butter

1/2 teaspoon vanilla
extract

MOCHA FUDGE

At our house, Peanut Butter Fudge was once the favorite.
I have to admit it's been displaced by Mocha Fudge.
If you like chocolate and coffee, this delight is for you.

1. Place the sugar, cocoa powder, and salt in a medium-sized saucepan, and stir to combine. Stir in the coffee.

2. Place the sugar mixture over medium heat, and cook, stirring occasionally, until it begins to simmer.

3. Turn the heat under the saucepan very low and cover. Allow to bubble for 3 minutes. Then remove the cover. This step will dissolve any sugar crystals and help insure a smooth and creamy finish.

4. Continue cooking until the mixture reaches 234°F to 238°F on a candy thermometer. Alternatively, cook to the soft-ball stage. To test, drizzle a little hot syrup into a cup of cold water. When the cooled syrup comes together when you roll it with one finger, it has reached the soft-ball stage.

5. Remove the saucepan from the heat, and add the butter and vanilla extract. Using an electric mixer, beat on high just until the syrup begins to thicken and starts to lose its shine. Quickly transfer the fudge to a buttered 8-inch pie plate or a similar pan.

6. Place the fudge in the refrigerator for about 10 minutes. Using a sharp knife, cut the fudge into squares while warm and serve.

COFFEE BEAN CLUSTERS

YIELD: 12–14 CLUSTERS

*These crunchy little clusters have a lovely,
lingering aftertaste that is quite delightful.
I confess to being hooked, and my taste
testers keep asking for more. Not a problem.
These clusters are ridiculously easy to whip up.*

I cup roasted
coffee beans

4 ounces German
sweet chocolate

1. Place the beans in a small bowl, and set aside.

2. Melt the chocolate according to package directions. Using a rubber spatula, combine the chocolate with the beans. Work quickly.

3. Lightly butter a large plate. Scoop the bean mixture up in heaping table-spoons, and place the clusters on the prepared plate. Allow to set before serving.

Conclusion

Nearly two thousand years ago, coffee was discovered by an Abyssinian goatherd and his frisky goats. Since then, the story of coffee has been one of astounding success. It seems as if nearly everyone has fallen in love with the tantalizing aroma and rich taste of coffee. In fact, worldwide, more than 400 *billion* cups are consumed each year. We drink it as a steaming espresso, as a frothy cappuccino, or as a plain old cup of Joe. We use it to flavor cakes, puddings, and candies. Most of us can't get enough of the enticing coffee bean.

Confessions of a Coffee Bean has been sheer joy from beginning to end. I can't tell you how much I have loved researching, writing, sipping, and munching my way through this book. I hope you have had as much fun reading your way through it, and that these pages have provided you with a greater appreciation of fine coffee. I also hope that I have inspired you to try some of the many wonderful coffee beans of the world, as well as some of the scrumptious accompaniments that you can prepare in your own kitchen.

Coffee is a passion with me. Now that you've read the confessions of a coffee bean, I hope that it becomes your passion, too.

ResourceList

For the true coffee lover, there's perhaps no more enjoyable activity than browsing through a specialty store and choosing wonderfully aromatic coffee beans or the perfect coffeemaker. But if there is no such store near you—or if you simply prefer to roam through catalogs and websites—this list will guide you to companies that offer a selection of fine coffees, good-quality coffee-making equipment, or other coffee-related products. And each of these companies will deliver your purchase to your door.

Café Connection
PO Box 460
Spring Grove, IL 60081
Phone: 800-711-4012
Website: www.thecafeconnection.com
Gourmet coffees, both regular and decaffeinated, including selected flavored coffees, plus gourmet coffee gift packs and single-serving packets.

Chef's Catalog
PO Box 620048
Dallas, TX 75262-0048
Phone: 800-884-CHEF
Website: www.chefscatalog.com
A wide range of equipment for coffee-making, including vacuum pots, plunger pots, coffee grinders, and cappuccino and espresso makers.

Dorothy McNett's Place
800 San Benito Street
Hollister, CA 95023
Phone: 831-637-6444
Website: www.happycookers.com

Thousands of quality pots and pans, cooking utensils, and gadgets, including the special pans needed to make Danish aebleskivers and an aebleskivers mix.

Gevalia Kaffe
Holmparken Square
PO Box 11424
Des Moines, IA 50309-1424
Phone: 800-GEVALIA
Website: www.gevalia.com

More than 30 varieties of coffee, including Jamaica Blue Mountain, Kona, and other select varietals, as well as many flavored coffees.

Gourmet Coffee Warehouse
671 Rose Avenue
Venice, CA 90291
Phone: 888-8-COFFEE
Website: www.lacoffee.com

Gourmet varietal coffees, both regular and decaffeinated; flavored coffees; and a selection of organically grown coffees.

Green Mountain Coffee
33 Coffee Lane
Waterbury, VT 05676-1529
Phone: 800-223-6768
Website: www.greenmountaincoffee.com

More than 60 varietals, flavored coffees, and decafs, as well as brewing equipment, coffee grinders, and more.

Jelks Coffee Company
PO Box 8667
Shreveport, LA 71148-8667
Phone: 800-235-7361
Website: www.jelks-coffee.com

Gourmet coffees, regular and decaffeinated, including a huge selection of flavored coffees.

Peet's Coffee and Tea
PO Box 12509
Berkely, CA 94712
Phone: 510-594-2100
Website: www.peets.com

A wide selection of coffee blends, single-origin roasts, and decaffeinated coffees, as well as brewing equipment, mugs, and sweet coffee accompaniments.

Starbucks Coffee
PO Box 3717
Seattle, WA 98124-3717
Phone: 800-STARBUC
Website: www.starbucks.com

All the famous Starbucks dark-roast blends, both regular and decaffeinated, as well as brewing equipment, grinders, and other accessories.

Torrefazione Italia
413 Pine Street, Suite 500
Seattle, WA 98101
Phone: 800-827-2333
Website: www.titalia.com

Eight distinctive Italian coffee blends, plus Italian pottery coffee service, dishes, and more.

Index

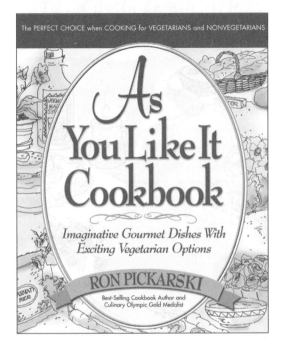

AS YOU LIKE IT COOKBOOK
Imaginative Gourmet Dishes with Exciting Vegetarian Options
Ron Pickarski

When it comes to food, we certainly like to have it our way. However, catering to individual tastes can pose quite a challenge for the cook. Have you ever prepared a wonderful dish, but because it contained beef or chicken, your daughter-in-law, the vegetarian, wouldn't go near it? To meet the challenge of cooking for both vegetarians and nonvegetarians alike, celebrated chef Ron Pickarski has written the *As You Like It Cookbook.*

Designed to help you find the perfect meals for today's contemporary lifestyles, the *As You Like It Cookbook* offers over 170 great-tasting dishes that cater to a broad range of tastes. Many of the easy-to-follow recipes are already vegetarian—and offer ingredient alternatives for meat eaters. Conversely, recipes that include meat, poultry, or fish offer nonmeat ingredient options. Furthermore, if the recipe includes eggs or dairy products, a vegan alternative is given for those who follow a strictly plant-based diet. This book has it all— delicious breakfast favorites, satisfying soups and sandwiches, mouth-watering entrées and side dishes, and delectable desserts.

With one or two simple ingredient substitutions, the *As You Like It Cookbook* will show you how easy it is to transform satisfying meat dishes into delectable meatless fare, and vegetarian dishes into meat-lover's choices. It will guide you in making culinary decisions that result in meals that are gratifying and delicious, and cooked exactly "as you (and your family) like them."

$16.95 • 216 pages • 7.5 x 9.0-inch quality paperback • Cooking • ISBN 0-7570-0013-4

THE SOPHISTICATED OLIVE
The Complete Guide to Olive Cuisine
Marie Nadine Antol

Simple. Elegant. Refined. It has truly evolved into a most sophisticated food. It is the olive. With a history as old as the Bible, the humble olive has matured into a culinary treasure. Enter any fine restaurant and there you will find the sumptuous flavor of olives in cocktails, appetizers, salads, entrées, and so much more. Now, food writer Marie Nadine Antol has created an informative guide to this glorious fruit's many healthful benefits, surprising uses, and spectacular tastes.

Part One of the book begins by exploring the rich and fascinating history and lore of the olive—from its endearing Greek and Roman legends to its many biblical citations to its place in the New World. It then looks at the olive plant and its range of remarkable properties, covering its uses as a beauty enhancer and a health provider. The book goes on to describe the many varieties of olives that are found around the world, examining their oils, flavors, and interesting characteristics. Part One concludes by providing you with everything you need to know to grow your own olive tree—just like Thomas Jefferson.

Part Two offers over one hundred kitchen-tested recipes designed to put a smile on the face of any olive lover. It first explains the many ways olives can be cured at home. It then covers a host of salads, dressings, tapenades and spreads, soups, side dishes, entrées, breads, cakes, and, of course, beverages to wind down with. So whether you are an olive aficionado or just a casual olive eater, we know you'll be pleased to discover the many new faces of *The Sophisticated Olive.*

$12.95 • 208 pages • 7 x 7-inch quality paperback • 2-Color • Cooking/Specific Ingredients/Olives • ISBN 0-7570-0024-X

**For more information about our books,
visit our website at www.squareonepublishers.com**